Ann's Evacuation Country Style

by

Deirdre Ann Yardley

Best wishes –
Ann Lambert (Yardley)

For my youngest sister, Jane, who knew nothing of these delights.

Living in the country during wartime was an experience not to be missed and, certainly, never to be forgotten by this city child.

CHAPTER I

1939 saw the Evacuation of St. Mary's Church of England Primary School, Churchill Road, Handsworth Birmingham. Hundreds of children of all ages were on the move all over the country, just as many parents were weeping for the decision they had made to bid a temporary farewell to their offspring – how long "temporary" might be was any man's guess! I suppose my mother's white and anxious face appeared and disappeared amongst the crowd on the pavement yet I do not recall it, for the picture vivid in my mind is of sitting on the "long" seat, downstairs, in a Birmingham Corporation bus with a gas mask slung around my neck. I suppose I must have had a card pinned to me indicating who I was, and where I lived, but the gas mask in its case was "the thing"! Never before had a Corporation bus parked in this quiet road outside our school. Never had one been filled with silent, straight-faced boys and girls, just waiting to go – where?

I was six. My two-year-old sister was undergoing almost continual treatment following the removal of a benign growth from her neck. She had had two operations within ten months. This treatment required visits to the hospital sometimes twice every day. The nurse had to put her hands either side of Elizabeth's jaws, lift her slightly off the ground and swing her sideways to stretch her neck muscles. This went on daily until one day there was a CRACK. This was what the nurses had been waiting for but what it did *I* had no idea.

During these visits I had to help Elizabeth to exercise her legs by showing her what to do having first had the exercises demonstrated to me. For instance, walking slowly, along a straight line on the carpet in the exercise room, barefoot, on the sides of the feet with toes curled round, and sitting down, picking up marbles with our toes and transferring them from a pile into a dish. Whatever I did Elizabeth copied. Mother always made sure we looked smart and the nurses referred to me as "Miss Tailor Made" – I even arrived wearing kid gloves.

It took Mother about an hour and a half to prepare Elizabeth for bed at night, bandaging, splinting, fitting a leather collar. On no account must she be allowed to cry, and on no account would she go to sleep! So it was Mother's lot to sit by her cot each night, holding her hand and singing to her till she fell asleep. Over and over again I would hear "I will give you the keys of my kingdom" till I could have sung it in my sleep. I can hear it even now. Anyone in such a predicament will understand the anguish when, whilst endeavouring to remove one's fingers from a lightly sleeping child's grasp, the slightest movement will bring a stir and a whimper and necessitate a further soothing lullaby. How often my mother's throat ached with the prolonged humming. Now, with me off her hands, she would have less worry. So might I have thought, looking back now through adult eyes – yet how her worry doubled in reality.

Me at 6 years old and Elizabeth at 2 years old just before evacuation.

4

Not one of those parents standing on the pavement knew where we were heading, but they were assured by our Headmistress, Miss Chandler, who accompanied us, that they would be informed before long.

This, for me, was the beginning of the most wonderful adventure.

The first recollection I have of my new surroundings was standing forlornly in a large classroom in the country school at Knighton-on-Teme, forty miles from home, where we were being herded into groups and handed over to a grown up. How we arrived here I have no notion – or how we left: perhaps tiredness was responsible for this lapse but, along with three other girls, none of whom I knew then and whose names I cannot now remember, I found myself in a house on a smallholding where I was destined to spend the next eighteen months.

Mr. and Mrs. Bournes' House

Mrs. Bourne was no stranger to guardianship and her kindliness endeared her to all who stayed under her roof. She stood no nonsense but who could be afraid when those blue eyes smiled down from out of her brown, weather-wrinkled face? She gave regular employment and shelter to girls from a Home, the eldest of whom, Selina, was shortly to leave. I do not remember much about them as I was only six years old.

As I looked around me I was observed by Mr. Bourne who was very quiet and shy and much shorter than his wife. He was ill at ease in company and preferred to remain in the background or disappear to his own domain – the orchard. There he stood, in a dim corner of the kitchen, his ruddy cheeks puffing away at his pipe, while his keen eyes followed my every movement. They had grown out of the ways of young children and must have been wondering whether they would be able to cope. Their faces were serious as they pondered over their new responsibility but any fears they may have harboured as to my homesickness or acceptance of the country way of life were soon to be dispelled. I fitted in as one born to this life.

There was no similarity between Anne of Green Gables and myself, yet I feel that I lived in her shoes – or almost! Mrs. Bourne was a replica of Marilla and Mr. Bourne was just another Matthew. With the help of her girls Mrs. Bourne kept her house as neat as a new pin. Approached from the road the wide brown gate opened onto the gravel drive between the grassed shrubberies. This led to the brown front door, centrally situated between flat sash windows but, do you know, I never remember that door being opened! That was the door to admit celebrities, to be opened to the most revered guest!

The window on the right of this door admitted light to the sacred room – the Best Room – for I suppose that was where the important visitors were received, but, like the front door, I never remember the room being used. I did once have the temerity to approach the door of the Best Room, tip-toeing towards it and glancing behind to make sure no-one was watching my daring action. I was eaten up with curiosity but as soon as the knob twisted in my hands and the gap widened sufficiently for me to peep inside a voice down the passage warned: "That's the Best Room. You're not allowed in there." I still wonder what it was really like inside for I was only able to gather a fleeting impression. Through the slit it appeared to be rather dim, smelling slightly musty and with dark leather furniture placed very precisely. Gracing the window was that plant of distinction – the aspidistra!

On the other side of the passage was the room where we had breakfast on a Sunday. Each Sabbath must have been identical for I remember only one. Dressed in my best dress and shining like a new pin I came downstairs and into this room. Oh, the smell of bacon and the sight of sausages which had been roasted in the oven so that the juice oozed out on to the plate! Before sitting down I was reminded to put on my pinafore: no marks must appear on Sunday clothes for, with extra additions to the household, washing must be kept to a minimum. I was ravenous and the smell made my mouth water with anticipation but breakfast could not be started until we were all at the table, all sparkling clean and dressed for Sunday with our pinafores on. I was growing impatient with hunger. "Do hurry up everybody," I kept saying over and over to myself in the hope that it would hasten their arrival. In due course we were assembled and, after grace, sat down to attack our food. No sooner had we started than our plates were empty. Breakfast did not last long enough. It was devoured in a flash. What a good job I had had to wait beforehand for I did at least savour it in anticipation! Hands had to be washed again after breakfast lest we should get grease on our clothes. Then came my big moment for which I had waited all week.

I sat for breakfast with my back to the door. On the wall opposite, which I had been facing since I came downstairs, was the range on either side of which was a tall cupboard. The right hand cupboard was the one which held my attention for in it was only one item, as far as I could remember, my watch. I must have been extremely fortunate to own a watch for it was treated like treasure. Was I the only child who possessed a watch, I wondered? It seemed ages that I had to wait for the meal to be cleared away before Mrs. Bourne would open those large cupboard doors. With great ceremony the knob would be turned and the doors swung open. There it rested, inside a glass tumbler, high on the third shelf, way out of my reach. Mrs. Bourne would take it out and very carefully set it to the right time. Then she would wind it up and slip it over my hand. The band was of corded silk which was tightened with a fascinating zipping sound before the fastener was clicked home very securely. From that moment I was inches taller in height and years older! I was wearing my watch and I was now ready for church! After the church service and before dinner off came my watch and back into the glass tumbler in the cupboard it went and there it was to remain until the same time seven days hence. Was this how watches were intended to be used?

The gravel drive which branched away from the front door wound round the house to the cobbled brick yard at the rear, a yard which was large and open with a hen run at the top and, further away, an orchard. But this clean-swept yard was overshadowed by a huge ramrod straight tree which even Jack's beanstalk would have had difficulty in outstripping. I have never seen such a tree. It was unique. In the early summer we waited daily for the happening and to the unwary this would be a missile from outer space hurtling towards its two legged object, intent on rendering it insensible. But the initiated would wait, open-armed, for green, egg-shaped fruits to fall and collect them before they hit the ground if possible as the impact would split their coverings. Today's sport is conkering but these were no chestnuts. These were unripe walnuts. Nowadays, walnuts come in hard, wooden shells which the children delight in cracking just for the joy of seeing what is inside, but these semi-soft fruits were green all through. It was many years later that I realised they were used immediately for pickling and not until ripe were they the walnuts with which I was familiar.

CHAPTER II

The Germans were about to attack and this was why we were removed from our homes to a place of safety. In order to confuse the expected but undesired visitors from abroad all indications telling them where they had arrived were to be removed, hence all signposts were rendered armless with just a black and white stump sticking out of the ground to remind the locals where to replace the arms when life returned to normal.

Fortunately, as it turned out, no enemy arrived to be confused, only mothers and fathers who had at last received news of our destination and had made plans to come and see us. Petrol was rationed but, with care, enough had been reserved to pay us a visit. Little did they realise how well we had been concealed and how long it would take to discover us. Parents were not told of our destination until we had been housed. They were dissuaded from visiting us for fear of unsettling us. But find us they did and this was to be the first of many weekly trips.

As fuel became more scarce agreements were reached for two, and later three, families, mine, Michael and Geoffrey Madden's and Sheila Henderson's, to travel together – "one week in our car, the next in yours and the third in theirs!" Our dark-haired teacher, Miss Raynor, began to question the regularity of these visits: "How is it you manage to come every week to visit your daughter with petrol so scarce?" was her frequent query, to which my father would reply: "Ah, Miss Raynor, that's my secret, but if there's anything you would like me to bring for you on my next visit I shall be very pleased to oblige." She was a special friend of mine from that moment.

So it was that every Sunday, after mid-day lunch, I would wait outside the gate for a car to come round the bend in the road. It was the only car which ever came along that road, or so it seemed to me. Like Toad of Toad Hall the sight of a motor car along those country lanes was something to be wondered at. Those roads were there solely for us to walk along or play in.

Outside the gate was a mound of chippings, a permanent mound of chippings, which was my hill on which to await the arrival of my family, Mother, Father and Elizabeth. It was put there ready for the winter so that when the ice and snow arrived a layer of grit scattered over the surface of the road would provide a grip for vehicles to bite into. If I ran up that mound once and down the other side I performed the same ritual a hundred times. How I wished they would come. Then joy, oh joy, they would arrive and the next hour or two would pass so quickly that all too soon it was goodbyes which were heard instead of hellos.

On several occasions I would be treated to a longer visit for my parents would come for lunch when Mrs. Bourne would provide a delicious rabbit meal for the princely sum of half-a-crown a head, 12½p in today's money. (In this way she could add a little to her meagre income.) Then afterwards we would go out for the afternoon around the country lanes, taking a picnic with us, so thoughtfully packed by Mother, and full of surprises. It was during this time that they were to learn of all my discoveries on my walks to school, flowers and animals which were new to me. These years in the country induced in me a love of nature.

When the time came to depart Mother would hand over a parcel of sweets to be shared amongst all the children in the house during the week. This was a wonderful gesture for sweets were rationed and could only be obtained in exchange for coupons. To Mother's and Father's coupons were added Grandma's allocation and by forfeiting all theirs they were able to treat us so generously.

It was strange how settled I became there. At school we all met to hear the tales – for example, how red-headed, hot-tempered Rita, who was living in the house with me, had torn all the wallpaper off her bedroom wall in her despair, how rude and unkind she was and how unhappy. She was removed and, I presume, sent back home.

As weeks passed and nothing untoward happened in connection with the war my friends began to drift back home too. Jean Walker from another house was no longer with us; Margaret Furnough longed for home and implored her parents to take her back with them, but me, I was the only one in the Bourne's household who stayed and I was in heaven.

Heaven was a log in the orchard. Here I could sit astride my steed, or side-saddle if I was more ladylike, and dream away the hours until I was called back to earth by a voice in the distance wondering how I had managed to elude them for so long and yet not be in any kind of mischief.

At the house end of the orchard, tucked away behind a hedge, was the hutch and its contents were a fascination for me. It stood on legs so that the wire front was at my eye level and there I would stand before it, winking back at the inquisitive pink eyes on the other side of the netting. Tempting indeed was the urge to put my fingers through the holes to stroke the soft, slinky, furry bodies as they undulated to and fro but I had sense enough to adhere to the warning frequently given. The ferrets were vicious! They had a purpose in life – to ferret out rabbits from their burrows so that Mr. Bourne could supply us with a nutritious rabbit pie or stew; but this activity was outside my comprehension. They reminded me so much of my angora rabbit which I had had at home and animals in hutches had always been pets before.

It was here, near the hutch, that the pig met his doom. Great preparations were made as soon as the day began and Mrs. Bourne's family arrived. Space was made in the kitchen, a clearing in the corner of the orchard was prepared and wood was stacked for a fire. Children were sent to play but all this activity was too much for our curiosity so, as undesirable onlookers, we were on the perimeter of the proceedings. The pig, with a rope around his neck, was dragged, pulled, urged and pushed alternately from the yard to the orchard, loudly squealing his indignation, as is a pig's prerogative. Titbits were paraded before his snout to entice this rotund beast to his slaughter whilst we stood in awe at a distance. It was not seemly for children to witness the rest of the execution so Mrs. Bourne's grandchildren and I sat outside in the orchard, but we guessed his throat was slit for before long the squealing ceased and wood smoke began to drift through the trees. Ah, his whiskers were being singed off. I will never know the butchering delights for at this point we were ushered from the scene of the crime: it was far too gruesome and our minds were at such an impressionable age. Little was it realised that curiosity and interest were far greater than tickled stomachs. This was living country-style, providing their own food, and we all enjoyed sausages for Sunday breakfast.

If you have ever had the good fortune to go into an outhouse where sacks of meal and corn are stored you will recall with pleasure the sweet odour mingled with the dusty smell of the sacking. It was my important duty to lift the latch on the door and wend my way inside through the stores stacked around the floor. The sack containing the maize for the hens was obvious – untied with the top half sagging over the side of the hard-stuffed bottom part. Lifting up the open end of the sack I would find the white enamelled pudding basin nestling inside waiting to be filled with the smooth golden nuggets of maize and near-round grains of corn. Careful not to spill any, I would make my way across the cobbled yard to the hen run where the rooster was the most fearsome spectacle I had to face. "Feed him and he won't feed on you," was the advice I had been given. It seemed to work. I loved to scoop out handfuls of corn and scatter it over the ground, watching the hens dash first to one patch and then another. If the cock so much as advanced a foot in my direction, though, I beat a hasty retreat to safety on the outside of the run for he was very fond of legs, particularly Mr. Bourne's trouser-covered legs out of which he one day pecked a beakful of material, causing quite a stir and not a few unmentionable words.

Eggs were always to be found in the nesting boxes at the rear of the hen house and carefully I would pick my way through the feeding hens jabbing their beaks at the ground, keeping a wary eye on the cock at the same time Shielding the eggs lest any should roll off the over-full basin I would manage to ease my way through the wire door, latching it safely behind me.

All this experience stood me in good stead for the days in the future when Father decided to try his hand at poultry farming. After returning to Birmingham, my father built a hen house and we had several hens and an aggressive cockerel. Each year eggs were hatched and fluffy yellow chicks lived in a coop on the lawn.

Me now 15 with baby Jane and Elizabeth now 11 on the hen coop in the garden of our house in Birmingham

I had joined the Girl Guides and one of the badges I earned was for Poultry Keeping. Each day my father commandeered the pressure cooker in the kitchen to cook all the potato peelings and food waste for the hens' mash and I had to mix it with bran and take it to them.

Girl Guide Poultry keeping badg

CHAPTER III

There were two ways which would take me to school, each a walk of just under an hour, and as there was no means of transport whatsoever, Shanks' pony had no competition. To the left, the road went in the direction of the Long Length - and a name more appropriately bestowed must yet be discovered. Straight stretches with nothing but hedges holds little interest for youngsters with no time to dally but the one magnetic attraction was Froggatt's pool.

The road to school took a sharp right turn at the beginning of the Long Length but by ignoring this corner and creeping ahead a few paces I would enter the mystic gloom of another world. The low branches of small spreading trees entwined overhead and the railings on either side of this narrow walk prevented me from falling into the pool below. Grit lay on the surface of the walkway indicating how seldom it was used and by silently creeping along, eerie echoes were prevented from sending prickles down my spine. Not a movement came from the pool, which boasted large water-lily leaves and beautiful wax-like flowers, but the sounds were magnificent. Frogs croaked from all sides, calling and answering each other. Such deep-throated croaks and so insistent were they that I felt almost able to understand their meaning and join in their assembly. I listened enthralled.

With a start a thought flashed through my mind – I'll be late for school! I had seen no other children; how time must have flown. If only my watch had not had to stand still in that glass tumbler on the third shelf of the large fireside cupboard! Even Dulcie Froggatt, whose father owned that wonderful pool, had not emerged from the "other side". Perhaps she had left before I had arrived. Dulcie was in my class and it was said her father kept a gamekeeper who always had a gun tucked under his arm. If he saw or heard me move in the green grotto I supposed he would immediately shoot off my head, mistaking me for a poacher. I must needs move quickly and noiselessly, fearing the worst

15

and breathing with short painful breaths lest I stir even a leaf before reaching safety down the right-angled turn of the road.

The other road was by far the most trodden and attractive one and on nine days out of ten I would be found dancing, skipping and swinging along it carrying my red, square oil-cloth bag dotted all over with white spots. Oil-cloth has a peculiar smell which lingers in the nostrils long after it is discarded – years afterwards, for I can smell it still. It must have been a forerunner of today's plastics. The said bag had two handles and had to be carried in the hand: there was no means of slinging it over my shoulder or carrying it on my back, which would have been a life-saver for me – or so I thought. Each day the contents were the same; a packet of sandwiches for my lunch (no-one ever had hot school dinners – not yet at least) and a half-pint glass bottle of lemonade. I am certain it was sherbet (we called it kali!) for the delicious nectar had to be home brewed. There was never a thought of buying lemonade as we now know it. Why, the nearest shop was a three-and-a-half mile walk away and the only tradesmen to call were the butcher and the baker who came in their very small vans just twice a week.

Happy to be alive I would travel this winding road meeting Michael and Geoffrey and the junior Bournes – very junior – from High Hall. Michael and Geoffrey were the next-door boys from home, evacuated like me. They stayed with the Williams in one of the two council houses which had recently been built down the road and how out of character these were amongst the old farms and cottages. (Mr. Williams was the R.A.C. man, who always seemed to be standing on the iron bridge near to school waiting to acknowledge any driver who entered his domain, welcoming them as potential clients.)

How I still blush to think of the day I had to kiss Geoffrey before all my friends! The long walk to school was relieved in many ways. Sometimes we would march along in time to the current popular tunes, singing at the top of our voices "Roll Out the Barrel", "Hang Out the

Washing on the Siegfried Line", or "Run Rabbit, Run Rabbit, Run, Run, Run". In the frosty weather we would stop now and then to smash the ice in the ruts with our heels or, if the ice covered a large enough area, we would spend as long as we dared sliding backwards and forwards till the ice wore out! This particular morning was "Truth, Dare and Promise" morning. We were almost at the top of Church Hill when it was my turn to choose. Usually I would take a promise as this was less likely to land me in trouble. With truth I might be forced to give away the secrets I held most dear, then life would be intolerable. Fingers would wag at me and torments would be thrown in my direction: I could never stand the misery. But this morning I was feeling rather bold: I would take a dare. Arms went round necks and heads bent in whispers while the darest of dares was cudgelled, then with smirking faces and glinting eyes, pronouncement was made. "We dare you to kiss Michael". Oh, the worst! I was mortified. Michael was a little older than me and it was so significant. I would have to marry him when I was older. Oh dear, that the earth would open up and swallow me. My knees shook. I felt sick. I would have to make an ultimatum. Now Geoffrey was younger and smaller than I was; there was nothing binding in choosing a younger person was there? "Please let me kiss Geoffrey instead," I pleaded. Ah, secrets were coming out; I could see their minds working. "That's fair," they agreed. After all, they now had meat for further torments. "Well, gather round then and hide me." So, once again, arms went round necks, but instead of heads bending low in conspiracy, eyes were now eager to see a dare earnestly performed. Geoffrey was quite obliging but, oh, the pain of that moment lived on for ages.

The very junior Bournes were the grandchildren of my guardians and there were four of them. We played together quite often and the youngest boy was the cause of my most terrifying moments. It was on one of those occasions when we were all in the "Sunday breakfast" room, idling around the table. It was too wet to be out of doors and we were wondering what to do when from the youngest grandson escaped an uncontrollable noise. Silence descended. Each looked at the others petrified lest he or she should be accused, but Grandpa Bourne knew the offender and considered strict action was demanded. Slowly he removed his leather belt. Slowly he advanced towards his grandson while the rest of us children jumped out of the path of the advancing admonisher. For the first time in my life I remember standing on the furniture, a leather sofa, with my back pressed against the wall, all ten fingers thrust in my mouth and eyes almost out of my head. As everyone else's eyes seemed to be on the same level I assume they too had found furniture on which to escape. A plague of rats scuttling over the floor could not have sent us up any higher. Grandson, and grandfather with strap menacingly held, moved around the table, the one viewing that object with relief, the other cursing its very existence.

"I'm sorry, Grandfather, don't strap me Grandfather, I won't do it again, let me go," and somehow that small boy disappeared backwards through the door and flew off home down the road to safety. It was several days before we saw him again and several minutes before we gradually stepped down to ground level eyeing every movement as the strap was refastened in its rightful place.

To return to the oil-skin bag – for this was the day I met neither the boys nor the Bournes nor anyone else en route. I had happily passed Amies' on the corner of the crossroads and had passed beneath the fine line of tall firs fronting the red Victorian rectory. How the wind whispered through those fir branches which, with an occasional "plop" would send a long, beautifully-shaped cone down to earth. Across the road was the first of two gates which led through to Mr. Adams' land. Everybody made sure that the gates were properly closed after they had passed through so that the animals would not stray. But strangely situated between these gates (which were about half-a-mile apart) was the church. As Mr. Adams owned the land and Mr. Adams lived in the farm alongside the church, I presumed the church was his also. The road through his property had no fences: we either walked on the tarmac or on his field or, better still, we used his cow dung pancakes as stepping stones.

Opposite his farm, at the side of the road, was a pear tree which showered down the most delicious pears, small, hard and sweet, a welcome bonus for our lunch-time bags. This morning was full of expectancy; there were bound to be some pickings for the taking. I reached the bend before the farm. There was the first sight of the tree, but, standing four-square in the road, guarding that tree, was the cow. "Like a red rag to a bull," flashed through my mind. "Like red oil-cloth", that is as near to "rag" as no matter. A cow won't know the difference. I stopped dead in my tracks. The cow stood dead in my tracks too, gazing with those huge brown orbs and chewing in anticipation of her meal to come.

"Help!" No sound came forth either from me or from my wished-for gallant knight. If I could hide my bag I could get past the obstacle but something must be done quickly before it realised I was carrying the dreaded "red rag". Perhaps if I hid the bag behind a bush I would be allowed to pass unattacked. But then I would have to forego my lunch and lemonade. If I walked nonchalantly on with the bag behind my back – but no, the cow would smell it. Stick it up my jumper – yes! That was the answer. I would then walk all round the field thus by-passing the dreaded beast.

Pears were forgotten in my anguish as I side-stepped delicately all around the field, frantically clutching the bottom of my bulging jumper, constantly facing the "ravaging bull", who turned not a whisker in my direction but continued to swish her tail and munch her cud whilst standing astride the road guarding the tree. Once in the region of relative safety I ran as I had never run before till I was through the gate at the other end and had slammed it shut behind me. I pleaded that I might carry another bag from then on and I prayed that the "bull" would never again meet me on that road. Oh, the perils that can befall an innocent are unbelievable!

Minus the presence of the cows, I loved that stretch of road for beside it stood the church.

Knighton Church

It was Mrs. Bourne's pride that every Friday she would polish till her arms ached and the lectern gleamed like burnished gold. The altar rails glinted in the sunlight and not a speck of dust remained in the pews: it could be seen in the coloured rays of sunlight streaming through the windows, its particles seeking a way of escape from the broad sweeps of her dusters! As the school bell declared the end of the week's lessons I would hurry along to the church, for that was where I would find her still, housemaid's overall donned, old felt hat pulled low over her tightly bunned grey hair, scrubbing her way over the tiles from altar to vestry, this the last chore of the day. I gingerly picked my way towards the organ, treading where the tiles had dried, careful not to step on the tombstone lest God should put a black mark on his list against my name. Or maybe it was because the person buried here below would be hurt if I trod on him – I would be. Whichever the reason, walking round the burial stone was like walking a tightrope; how did older, fatter people manage? There was hardly enough room for small folk like me.

The Nave of Knighton Church

The Nave of Knighton Church showing the gravestone

When scrubbing was completed and everywhere gleamed to Mrs. Bourne's satisfaction, we left silently by the only door, securely locking it behind us, safe in the knowledge it was ready to receive its Sunday worshippers.

I loved those Sunday services. I sang the hymns. I knelt for prayers. It was grand down below. No-one could see me playing with my glove fingers or fiddling with my watch. I counted the buttons on my coat and wondered how many holes there were in all the buttons added together. By twisting around I could even count those on the back belt – but too late, it was time to stand up to sing again. The sermon time was a delight indeed but the vicar's utterances fell on stony ground! I preferred to dream my own dreams which had so much more meaning. Occasionally a word became mixed in my thoughts which had no right to be there and made nonsense of my sentences – but there, I'd have to begin thinking all over again.

At last it was time to leave and shake hands with the minister, the Reverend Randle, who waited outside the door in the sunshine. He beamed his good mornings to all his flock; but what else did he do during the week was a thought which flashed through my mind as my eyes met his in acknowledgement. Each time I walked past the rectory I would stare in awe at the façade. Never did I see a soul go in or come out. Yet it was behind that oak front door that I guessed that ladies in their best hats sat to take afternoon tea. No matter how hard I looked I could not visualise the scene through those red bricks but perhaps one day I would be a lady of enough consequence to join that elite circle.

CHAPTER IV

Christmas came but once while I was billeted here and I suppose it was as festive then as now. Mrs. Bourne was a wonder considering she must have been quite elderly, for this Christmas she also entertained her daughter, Edith, and family who lived away in Birmingham and came not only for Christmas Day but for the whole festive season.

Two of Mrs. Bourne's three grand-daughters had to share my back bedroom. It was always a dim room as I remember but their presence made it gloomier than ever. I was the odd one out. This was their grandmother's house and I was an outsider. I had no right to be there and they assumed possession. It was Christmas Eve and excitement reigned. They discussed what they were to have and what they hoped to find in their stockings next morning. My hopes were listened to with only half an ear. I had so wanted a party dress but this was out of the question. My clothes had to be dark and sensible so as to last as long as possible between washings. Even my outdoor clothes were sensible – and drab! – navy blue coat which came below my knees to allow for growth and navy blue velour hat, deep-crowned and wide brimmed. I was a miniature edition of Freddy "Parrot-Faced" Davis, who appeared in the 60s on our television screens as a comic to entertain the children.

Me in my hat and coat with Elizabeth and a friend

This night was the night when children did not go to sleep, to the consternation of Father Christmas, and, true to custom, I slept with one eye open. At a very late hour the latch on the bedroom door was softly raised and by the light of the dim bulb outside on the landing I could see Mrs. Bourne's head peeping round the door. "Goodnight, God Bless," she whispered. It wasn't Father Christmas after all. I must have grown too sleepy to wait for him any longer but by four o'clock the next morning he'd been and gone. A giant black and white panda for Freda, Mrs. Bourne's granddaughter, sat on the bed next to mine and the ecstasy with which he was greeted was a welcome indeed. But there on the back of the bedroom door, hanging on a hanger with a note attached, was a party dress for me. It was royal blue taffeta, over-checked with pencil lines in red and black, with short puffed sleeves. Oh, how it rustled when I took it down. My mother knew just what I wanted after all. I cared not for any other delights. Christmas would remain with me for every minute that I wore that dress. It surely was a dream come true.

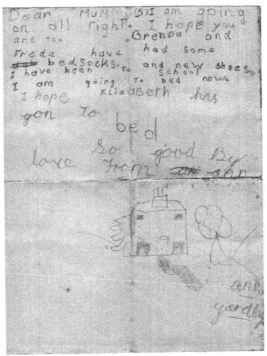

A copy of one of my letters home

Anxious for us to enjoy as happy a Christmas as possible some of the mothers and fathers of children still out here in the country had put their heads together and planned a surprise. And what a surprise it turned out to be. It was arranged that we would be collected from our places of residence and taken to The Talbot Hotel, a public house down on the main road near to the school, in time for the mid-day meal on Christmas Day.

The Talbot Hotel

What a sight greeted us as we went up the steps and through the front door. All the parents who had been able to participate, including my parents with Elizabeth, had arrived earlier that morning laden with goodies and gifts. During the past weeks they had saved their coupons (for now food was strictly rationed) and had gradually gathered together the luxuries which are an essential ingredient of any party. There was a tree decorated with lights and baubles which someone had thoughtfully brought from home and packages and parcels of all sorts and sizes were piled around the base. So attractive was the array that the eager-eyed would-be recipients endeavoured to guess what each parcel contained.

Games were arranged for the afternoon and then, after tea, Father provided further entertainment. He had managed to borrow a projector and screen and had hired several rolls of film, among which were Mickey Mouse films, and for the rest of the evening we sat enthralled while he gave us a film show.

The celebrations came to an end with our departure at nine o'clock after a most wonderful and unexpected day with our families. It was too late for most of them to return to the city so they had booked up there for the night and we looked forward to seeing them again on the morrow before they returned home.

As the weeks passed into spring I derived more and more enjoyment from living here in the country. For days now I had plagued the life out of Mrs. Bourne's grand-daughter, Monica, from High Hall, who was older than me and had a big bike. "Please let me have a go. Please will you teach me to ride?" So, without any feeling of danger, I was sat upon the saddle and was told to "go straight" while she held the saddle at the back. We were between high hedges on a hump in the road and, as I was told to go straight, straight I went, straight into the under hedge on the other side of the road. Monica didn't realise before that the road just here had a curve in it. It had never been a problem to her. Again and again I sat upon the saddle up on the hump in the road learning to "go straight" and balance and at last the day came when my family, on their weekly visit, were to be informed of my prowess.

"Mummy, I can ride a bike. You must come and see me." Out of the house we went and set off along the road. Mother's face was full of bewilderment and Father wore a smirk which meant "a strange daughter we have here!"
"But I thought you were going to show us how you could ride a bike."
"Yes, I am."
"But where it is? You haven't one."

Well, of course I hadn't. We were walking to it! Past High Hall we walked to the hump on the road where Monica just happened to be standing with her bike. Light was beginning to dawn on my parents' faces. "Please can I have a ride, Monica?" I asked, and again we went through the now familiar routine. She held the saddle, I mounted, and away I sailed down the hump. If only I had seen the horror on my mother's face! My legs weren't long enough for my feet to touch the pedals so they were tucked up on the frame and the use of brakes was unknown to me. But I could go straight – at least keep in the centre of the road. Along I bowled until the slope gave out and the bicycle came to a halt. I managed to step off before the bike fell clattering to the ground. By this time I was out of sight but the noise of the falling bicycle had indicated the worst to my mother. As she came running round the bend expecting to see the victim in a heap in the road, I came running back to her wreathed in smiles. "Did you see me? I can ride it, can't I? Please can I have a bike now?" But several months were to elapse before it was deemed safe for me to possess one of my own.

High Hall

There had been much behind-the-scenes activity while I was enjoying my first taste of country life. Through great perseverance and a lot of attention from doctors and nurses and daily massage and exercises, both at the hospital and at home, my sister, now four years old, had progressed sufficiently for a recommendation to be made that a spell in the country would be most beneficial. And so I learned that my father had taken a cottage in the vicinity, about a mile and a half distant from the Bournes' smallholding. I was soon to be in my second heaven!

The first recollection I have of this transfer is the night of the removal – not of household goods but of me. It must have been at the end of a day of hard work for my parents for my father was a furniture remover and it was therefore very much a "do-it-yourself" job. But just when the time and inclination had come for him to sit down with his feet up for that very well-earned rest his thoughts were elsewhere – "I'll have to fetch her before she's too tired." As the removal van was now parked, it was unthinkable to use it as transport to fetch an eight-year-old girl who was strong in limb and stout in heart so his weary feet trod the distance to fetch me, knowing full well he would have to retrace his steps without a break.

I was ready and waiting, packed and impatient. Goodbyes and thanks were said but, of course, I wasn't going far away. I would see them all soon. Then we set off for my new home. Father carried my luggage – one minute hand case – and I desperately tried to keep in step with him as we marched through the silent darkness. Not a car or bicycle passed us. No-one on foot was astir save us two brave souls. Not a gleam of light showed from anywhere for the whole country was in blackout.

The drone of a plane overhead made my heart sink for every plane was an enemy to me. How anyone could possibly tell the difference between ours and the enemy by listening to the engine sound alone I just didn't know. At that time Father was a smoker and, as we walked in silence, my eyes were riveted to the glowing end of his cigarette. "Daddy don't you think the Germans will see the light from your cigarette and know we're here?" I managed to whisper, imagining them looking out of the windows of the plane above, anxious to drop a bomb on any moving object. "No, you're safe with me," was his reassuring reply, but I was only partly reassured. I felt much happier as we walked past the van, through the five-barred gate, under the cherry trees and into the cottage which brought me again into my own family circle.

ABC was how our new home came to be known. Officially logged as Aston Bank Cottage it became abbreviated within weeks for, as with all things dear, an affectionate nickname is soon bestowed. The living room was unevenly tiled, the small downstairs "guest room" smelt musty, the kitchen had a brown cement sink and we cooked by a fragile Calor gas stove with two small rings on top. The stairs were uncarpeted and the few that there were twisted spirally ending in one large bedroom the floor of which sloped towards the window at the side of the cottage. From this bedroom a latched paling door opened to a smaller room. This cottage had character! The outside appearance was of a black and white timbered dwelling, bungalow-like with a corrugated iron roof. Originally this roof was thatched but as the thatch wore out the owner, always loath to part with his money, opted for the cheaper repair and, instead of incurring a costly bill by re-thatching, he covered the existing one with the corrugated iron. As it now stood it insulated the dwelling and proved exceptionally soundproof for one never heard even the largest hailstones falling on it and could never determine the state of the weather simply by listening for the noise of the elements.

ABC with Dorothy, Elizabeth and me

Mornings from now on began at around six o'clock. My father was no longer with us as he had work to do back home. I had promised to look after my mother and sister and would do that to the best of my ability. So I was the alarm clock for the family. With regularity, like clockwork, whether summer or winter, I would creep stealthily down the stairs endeavouring to prevent the creaks and groans which always brought them to life. I must have been unnatural in that my first occupation was to wash! Now there was no tap anywhere in the house from which to acquire water. This had to be fetched from outside. With bowl in hand along the passage I would go to the stout front door which I would unlock as quietly as possible. Outside this front door, right in the centre of the path, stood the pump. At this point all thought of sleeping persons disappeared. After all, there were only two who could possibly be affected since there were no other living souls within earshot. It was with great joy that I raised the pump handle and then pushed it down again. After repeating this process several times it worked. With great wheezes on the upward movement and greater squeals of delight on the downward stroke the pump joyfully gushed forth its precious bounty which splashed and spattered as it tried,

31

sometimes successfully and most times hopefully, to aim it in the bowl on the ground below. With a dripping bowlful of sparkling, ice-cold water, I returned to the kitchen to strip and give myself an all-over, stand-up bath. Mother often tells how she came downstairs from her night's sleep to find me standing naked in a bowl of water, bluer than the bluest washing powder and yet I never caught cold.

As you may already have suspected, no bathroom existed with hand basin, or bath, except for the tin variety which was hanging up on a nail outside the front door! If we were really desirous of a bath the tin monstrosity was brought in and placed before the fire in the living room. Several kettles of water were needed to give us sufficient depth to reap any benefit and the first water to be poured into the bath was inevitably cold by the time the next kettleful was ready. It was hardly worth all the effort. The toilet was way round the back of the house and was reached only after a slow or fast approach, depending on the urgency, along the narrow path three-quarters of the way round the cottage.

After a warming breakfast I would set off from home for my hour's trek to school. ABC stood in the middle of a cherry orchard. To walk beneath those trees when they were loaded with sweet-smelling white blossom was bliss, or to kick through the petals as they drifted to the ground was like kicking up confetti strewn hundreds of yards after the most noble of society weddings. Later in the year of course we had watched the small, hard, green fruits ripening to their red and yellow splendour, a variety of cherry little seen in the shops nowadays. These large, fat, juicy, red and yellow fruits – almost like miniature apples – were so much sweeter than the dark red cherries sold in the greengrocers' shops and when the picking time arrived how I envied those men and women with large, strong baskets slung on their arms, lost amongst the branches of the trees. When the baskets became too heavy to hold, or the cherries had to be reached for, the baskets were slung from the rungs of the ladders by a metal hook and when the basket was full it would be placed alongside other equally full baskets around the base of the trees. Weighing would be carried out in the orchard on a huge spring balance hooked to one of the lower tree branches and when adjudged to be of the correct weight and the cherries of a good standard a cardboard cover on which was printed the name and address of the farmer would be fixed under the handle covering the entire top of the chip in which the cherries were now packed ready for transportation to the market. (A chip was a cardboard basket.) Calls could be heard at regular intervals from some of the lady pickers: "Could you move my ladder please?" and the said ladder would progress around the tree. Many's the time I would have one foot on the bottom rung desirous of mounting to the height of at least one cherry but I had to be content with those which warned me of their presence by hitting me on the head first.

An accompaniment to this industry was the tinkling of tin foil strips dangling from the trees and catching the sunlight. This was one method employed by the farmer in his attempt to prevent the thieving of his crop by the feathered inhabitants. Left unchecked, they would soon strip the branches of the fruit. Another method was the use of clappers which the farmer would shake vigorously on his trips through the orchard. But in case these attempts failed, for birds are wily creatures, a device was planted in the trees and timed to go off at regular intervals during the daytime. It sounded for all the world like gun shots. The birds soon grew accustomed to these sounds too and continued their thieving unperturbed, unaware of the approaching farmer with his gun. He would drive his empty van into the orchard and depart with the back laden. Wood pigeons were the biggest menace and the number of cherry stones blocking their gullets was a sight which had to be seen to be believed.

Auntie Cis (my Godmother) Elizabeth, Mother and me in the cherry orchard

Over the stile and down the meadow to the gate and stile at the bottom and I would be out on the road at the beginning of Jewkes Lane. What a place to be in the winter with the weight of the snow bowing down the branches of the trees. I would trudge through the snow where nothing had passed before, where every footprint made was mine and all the ground before me lay undinted. The drips from the branches all around were the only accompaniment to my crunching steps and, as the warmth of the sun began to melt the snow, trickles of water would be heard making their way to the brook.

Half way along Jewkes Lane, on the right, was a copse sloping down from the road to the brook below and it was here where I was led astray. My approach must have surprised, but not frightened, a young rabbit for, before my nose, he bounded away into the copse. I followed as fast and noiselessly as I dared but he had been instructed in the art of evasion for I quickly lost sight of him. However, I now knew where he had his residence and after school that day I recounted my experience to my mother.

"I did try to catch him but he wouldn't wait," I explained.

"You hadn't got the right method, dear," said my mother.

"Oh, hadn't I? Then what is the right method?"

"You must take a little bit of salt with you then creep up quietly behind him. When he's not looking sprinkle a little bit on his tail and he'll be quite ready then to let you pick him up."

The next morning I left for school clutching my dribble of salt in a little bit of greaseproof paper, the top twisted tightly so that it wouldn't spill and so that I'd have a sort of handle to hold it by. I couldn't get to the copse quickly enough. On reaching it at last I sat down on the grass to wait. The sun shone warmly. I waited patiently. I waited. I waited impatiently, untwisting and twisting the top of the small packet in my hand. I began to lay a trail of salt in the grass but, alas, the rabbit knew of my plan and was playing safe. He never appeared again. How my mother has since laughed but I knew my kindness was better than salt for I did catch my rabbit – not this one but a younger relative.

This morning I was late for school, which was not surprising since there were so many distractions for inquisitive eyes on the whole length of the route. There were no children around for, unknown to me, they had arrived at school at least ten minutes earlier. I was within a few hundred yards of the building, almost at the top of Church Hill, and my eyes were roving over the right hand bank at the roadside. During the winter, in the icy weather, this hill was unnavigable – or nearly so.

Many's the time I have almost reached the summit only to miss my footing and slide right down to the bottom again on the ice. In order to be certain of reaching the top we would have to walk with our feet at an angle against the soil of the bank, gripping the tufts of grass to help us along. It was a strenuous effort and we would arrive at school on such days as this with noses streaming, eyes gleaming and cheeks a rosy red. Gloves would be soggy and muddy and often knees sore and bleeding but once in school our clothes would be strewn around the fire-guard which guarded the huge anthracite stove – there was one in each of the three classrooms – the only means of heating the building.

As I said, I had almost reached the top of the hill, eyes scanning the bank, when a movement caught my eye. It was the most infinitesimal movement – the blinking of an eyelid. There, basking in the sunshine, filling one of the many holes in the bank, was the dearest, the cutest baby rabbit I'd ever seen. He wasn't an intelligent infant for he'd ignored all his mother's early teachings. I stroked his wuffling nose and very gently lifted him out of his burrow. Cradling him in my two hands I carried him as fast as was humanly possible considering my precious cargo straight into my classroom and to the teacher standing behind her desk. Never heeding the interruption I was causing I glowed with pride and wonderment as I carefully opened my hands to reveal the soft furry bundle which seemed to be not in the least bit afraid. He rather revelled in the admiration. All the children in the class gathered round with their "Let me see," and after all had surveyed I was told to take it to show the headmaster who was teacher of the top class in the room next door. He was delighted and so was his class. Would I please go and show the infant class? With the rounds completed I went back to my own teacher. "What shall I do with it now, Miss Raynor?"
"Well, it is such a baby, it will be missing its mother. I think you should take it back and replace it exactly where you found it."
So, proudly, I walked out of school back to the bank where I placed the dear little bundle in exactly the right rabbit hole. At least, I think it was exactly right for, of all those there in the bank, this was the one the rabbit ran down so it must have been his right home. It was after ten

o'clock that morning when I actually sat down in my desk but work never entered my head at all that day.

CHAPTER VI

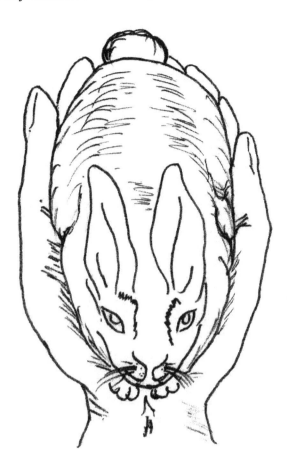

Knighton School (now a private house)

School was the happiest of places for me, except on that one morning when the Headmaster walked through our classroom door. As he appeared I was standing directly in front of him, for it was during a geography lesson, and I was reading my passage aloud to the class. There were relatively few children in the school, therefore they were of a wide age range in each of the three classes and, although I was only nine, I was amongst the older juniors sitting in the end row. I was considered clever enough to twice take the entrance exam – we called it The Scholarship – for admittance to Worcester or Kidderminster High Schools but I was, twice, not clever enough to pass it! However, my consternation was so great when the Headmaster entered to find me reading aloud that I made an inexcusable error of pronunciation, such a slight error that I doubt whether he thought again about it, but to me it was so dreadful that I blushed to the roots of my hair. It made me look so small amongst the older juniors with whom I had to keep my place. I had reached the bottom of the page and as I turned over to continue I glanced up at his entrance. My eyes had caught the pattern of the word but the Headmaster's presence had removed all comprehension of the passage and I ended up reading, before all the others, about "the hot

Julee sun". "That doesn't sound right. Let me see," said the all-important gentleman who had such faith in so small a being. I turned the book round so that he need not read it upside down (a skill which I later mastered as a teacher in my own right!) and he laughed as he handed it back to me. "The hot **JULY** sun. You must learn to read properly" was his mortifying comment. Oh, that I could be rendered invisible. Isn't it strange what an insignificant incident will do to a sensitive child!

Another lesson I recall was a nature lesson in which we had to draw and colour a celandine. Celandines proliferated in all the hedgerows.

It was around this time that I had my first lesson in First Aid. School stood at the top of the hill and the wind blew all around. As we walked along this high ridge of road the telegraph wires sang above our heads. "Someone's having a long conversation this morning." We discussed who it might be for that was the only reason in our minds for the wires to be humming so loudly. That it was the wind whistling through them never entered our heads. In fact, in order to eavesdrop on the conversation we would stand right up against the telegraph poles, our ears pressed close against the wood in anticipation of listening in on the talk!

This morning the wires were positively buzzing and windows and doors rattled. The doors inside school were wide and solid but the one into the Headmaster's classroom had six small glass panes in the top half. We were hard at work when there was a terrific bang followed by a shattering of glass then silence. A gust of wind had caught that door, slamming it shut with such ferocity that the walls shook. We did not know just then that Pat's first finger had caught the brunt of the impact. We later saw her sitting, white-faced, and holding her arm high above her head with a very bloody bandage wrapped around her fist. Every time her arm dropped with aching she was urged to hold it higher. The tip of her finger was almost severed and before long she was to be whisked off to the cottage hospital where it was stitched back in place. From that day to this I have been waiting for the opportunity to tell someone that in such an incident, by holding one's hand above one's head, less blood will be lost as it will drain back to the heart but, Heaven knows, I hope I will never have to pass on this information in practice. For weeks after, Pat's finger was bandaged to an immense size but the stitching was a success. I doubt whether she ever thinks about it now.

Morning break came as a most welcome diversion. At the appointed time the Headmaster's wife came along from the School House, which was built adjoining the school proper. She was carrying a large tray on which were three giant-sized jugs of steaming hot cocoa. There was one jug for each class and she came in and placed ours on the tin tray set out ready with yellow pottery beakers, one for every child. One at a time we would leave our desks to fetch the drink which Miss Raynor carefully measured out for us from the jug. It was far too hot to drink but while waiting for it to cool we would curl our fingers around the beaker to warm them. Winter mornings were wonderful with this special treatment to look forward to. I suppose we enjoyed our milk in summer just the same for it certainly cooled us down on those long hot days which seemed to abound at this time.

Everyone was urged to do their bit towards the "War Effort", man, woman and child, no matter what age. My father was fortunate in that he did not join one of the services, although he did his stint as a "firewatcher" and as a member of the "special police". Knowing that, as a furniture remover, my father had large vans available, a relative who worked in a sheet metal firm which made parts for aircraft contacted him and asked if he would work on contract for them as they were not having much success with their present arrangements. After due consideration my father and his brother agreed to the proposal and from then on they were working for the Ministry of Aviation. All the sign writing on the vans had to be deleted and in its place, in small insignificant lettering, was written their registration number. No-one was to know what they were transporting, where to or where from. My father's journeyings took him from Birmingham to Bristol and back, generally twice and sometimes three times a week, and occasionally the run was northwards to Accrington, each time carrying aeroplane parts – bulk heads and shoulder cowls – from manufacturer to aircraft factory for assembly. Since there were restrictions as to his routes he was unable to come home every night. He endeavoured to be at ABC mid-week and, mostly on Wednesday but sometimes on a Thursday, we would receive a message telling us to expect him at a certain time that evening. We had no telephone; the nearest one was at the farm owned by the farmer from whom we had rented the cottage, so we had to rely on him to accept and remember to pass on any such calls. This he did in his own good time! But at week-ends, from Saturday night till Sunday evening, we could always expect Father to be with us. Tales of his travels and experiences were listened to with delight. It was as though he moved in another world.

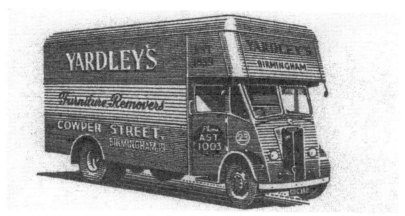
Father's Guy van

The words "War Effort" were no strangers to us in school either. The teachers must have seriously considered our capabilities for they hit upon an excellent idea. We all had to do a knitting sample during the afternoon devoted to craft activities – all the girls that is! I had learned to master the art when I was four years old and suffering from a bout of boredom! Measles had struck the house and I had been very poorly, at one time delirious, but had recovered enough to want something to do. I was out of bed, dressed, but not allowed out of the bedroom. You see, my sister, who was less than a year old, was in the next bedroom recovering from the first of two major operations and it was imperative that she should be kept as far away as possible from all infection. When I did creep along the landing I was most impressed by the large white sheet which had been wrung out in disinfectant and pinned up over her bedroom door and the white enamel bowl of water and disinfectant standing before it on the floor. Only Mother and the doctor passed through this doorway and at each entrance the washing of hands took place in an effort to minimize the danger of spreading the disease. The problem of finding an activity for a lonesome convalescent was soon resolved. A stout pair of knitting needles, a ball of wool and my own small armchair placed before the gas fire intrigued me. I was shown the rudiments of knitting and, with tongue in cheek, or lips pursed with the effort, it took only a few days before Teddy was decked out in a brand new scarf.

So it was that my sample square of knitting was a very creditable piece of work. In company with the older girls, I was allowed to make my choice: a balaclava or a pair of socks. When finished they were to be sent to men in the services. I had seen my mother knitting my father's socks and indeed the General's Lady, Lady Edith, who lived at Maes Court, always walked round the roads knitting socks, and I was fascinated by the process of going round and round using four needles instead of two so, young as I was, I proudly stated I would knit a pair of socks. Miss Raynor's eyes seemed to see through to my innermost soul. Perhaps she hadn't heard me. "Please may I have my wool?" Slowly, wonderingly, she handed me a hank of dark grey wool which she took from the huge bag standing beside her desk. Nowadays children are given bright, attractive colours to make their work more interesting but of course soldiers couldn't wear such brightly coloured socks! I found someone to hold my hank while I wound it. Then I selected my four needles and asked Miss Raynor how I should start. I must have been quite a headache! But I did enjoy doing my war work for these proved to be the first of many such articles I was to knit. First the welt, straight for the leg, turn the heel, straight again for the foot as far as the toe, then, with only the final decreasing left to do, I had almost finished one sock. One more to do and there was my perfect pair of socks. I was so proud. My name was written on a label and this was pinned to the socks, then they were added to the growing pile of articles waiting to be parcelled up and despatched. And that was the end of my war effort. It was months later that Miss Raynor handed me an envelope. I opened it and couldn't believe my eyes. There inside was the letter, written to ME PERSONALLY, from Arthur, a sailor in the merchant navy. He had worn my socks and had written to tell me he thought they were beautiful. How I've wished and wished that I had written back to Arthur. How I now wish I had kept this letter for who knows what may have happened to him? I had reached my Seventh Heaven sooner than I thought!

My knitting activity progressed. I could make something for myself, so I chose to make a jumper in salmon pink, a hideous colour which suited me not one jot, but, to me, it was delightful. This work I could take home with me in a bag to do in my spare time in the evenings. And how I loved those evenings when we would sit beside the fire in the lamplight listening to the wireless or reading or knitting. Mother would sometimes stop doing her socks for a short while and peel, slice and dice a quarter of a raw swede which we would then munch instead of apples, for at this time food was seasonal and not nearly so plentiful as we are used to having now. However, it was the time between leaving school and reaching home when that knitting bag containing my salmon pink work came into its own!

I was still intrigued by the language of love as croaked in the land of the frogs but, whereas the Froggatt's Pool frogs belonged to the noble class, those in the Jewkes Lane pool were a common lot! No mysterious surroundings for them, just an open pool at the side of the road, accessible to all and sundry who cared to crawl beneath the barbed wire around the perimeter. I was one of these! The amphibians here were not nearly so vociferous. Maybe they were wary of the moorhens who paddled to and fro', necks jerking at each movement, just like a mechanical toy, as they sought amongst the reeds for food. But if the frogs made less noise they made up for it with greater activity for this pool was overloaded with spawn. With toes squelching in the mud and knees almost buried in it, I would have my nose practically in the water looking for the tadpoles in all their stages of development. With fingers parted I drove my hands into the water and lifted them out with a sucking noise. The spawn would ooze and drip through my fingers, plopping back into the pool. What a marvellous experience! I did this repeatedly till, so obsessed with my pastime, I felt I couldn't leave it all behind. But what should I do? I had no jam jar. I scouted round but there were no rusty old cans to be found. Then my eye alighted on my knitting bag which I had parked on the grass verge. Out came the salmon pink jumper and pins. Wool and knitting were stuffed into any pockets which would accept them, regardless of the loss of innumerable stitches. The bag was the receptacle I had been looking for. Handful after handful of the slimy, jelly-like substance was stuffed into the cotton bag and, when there was no room left to spare, I decided that was the time to head for home. The bag was heavy, water was beginning to drip through the fabric and the sloppy stuff wouldn't keep still but, with great endeavour, I reached home intact. Jam jar after jam jar I filled while my mother became more and more horror struck. She was already ahead of me, seeing the developing frogs becoming a plague to overrun our property, but although it never reached the proportions she envisaged, she was certainly endowed with foresight!

Jewkes Lane was a continual source of wonder and delight. Behind the tall hedge was a triangular-shaped field which in springtime was smothered with bloom upon bloom of crocuses, golden yellow, blue to purple and white. There was not even room to place a foot between them without squashing several of the heads. It always surprised me that the colour was so deep in the petals yet the stem was so white as though drained of all its strength. The sight evoked in me a feeling which must have been akin to Wordsworth's when he saw his "host of golden daffodils". Further down the lane and on the opposite side towards the pool was the summer haunt of the dragonflies. With bodies at least six inches long and brilliant blue and green double wings they looked like miniature bi-planes hovering amongst the honeysuckle in the hedge. In a flash they were gone to divebomb over the pool, feeding on smaller winged insects which rose only a few inches above the surface of the water. This must have been my favourite spot as Mother would no doubt agree.

Mrs. Amies' house

Each day on my way home I had to call at Mrs. Amies'. This was the house at the crossroads where Jewkes Lane led on to the road from Bournes, where I stayed, and High Hall, where the Bournes' grand-children lived, to Maunds farm and, in due course, to the main road to Tenbury. This was a lovely sheltered corner where the sun streamed down onto a high bank of short, straw-like grass. At the right time of the year I knew that I would find wild strawberries growing on that bank and, if I were first there, the sight of those delicious small, red fruits was too great for me to pass them by. My reason for calling at Mrs. Amies' house was to collect a daily quart of milk. Each morning I would call on the way to school to leave the empty can and each evening I would collect it filled. There was a lid which fitted tightly on top but it was on these occasions I discovered that if I removed the lid and held firmly to the handle I could swing the can of milk round and round like the arms of a windmill and, even at a height high above my head, the milk can upside down, no milk would fall out. I was puzzled. By going slower and slower it got more chancy but I was so adept at the windmill game that I never lost a drop!

On reaching the pool my distraction was complete and, hey presto, I would disappear. The only indication of me ever having been present in the area was a quart can of milk standing alone in the centre of the road. By this time Mother would be wondering how much progress I had made on the homeward journey and, on a pleasant afternoon, would take it into her head to come and meet me. From the brow of the hill she would receive the message "am around somewhere," sent via the solitary object gracing the middle of the road. Oh, it was quite safe as regards traffic - there wasn't any. Taking several minutes to reach the can she would be straining her ears to catch any sound of distress but none was to be heard. Instead a head would pop up from underground with the breeziest of "hellos". I had found a tunnel. As a guard against flooding a fairly large pipe had been placed below the road to drain away excess water from the pool to the field on the other side and, in summer when the water was low, only a trickle ran through, thus allowing me to bend double and ease my way from one side of the road to the other underneath it! Whatever next?

CHAPTER VII

I was a welcome visitor in those early days to Mrs. Amies' corner house. She always greeted me with a smile, her bird-like eyes behind steel-rimmed spectacles darting here and there as she bustled to supply me with the milk. On other occasions I would go specifically to play with Sheila Henderson (whose father's car was the "theirs" of the weekly Sunday visits) and Mrs. Amies' other boarder, Betty Albeard, who was my age and often came to play at ABC.

Elizabeth, Betty Albeard, Sheila Henderson and me on a log

When visiting with my mother I would pass through the front gate and walk up the path to the front door which overlooked the garden at the back! Its porch was smothered in a profusion of purple clematis which always seemed to be accompanied by a cloud of flying insects.

The front of Mrs. Amies' house

Adult experience has explained this phenomenon as my own clematis appears to attract my own share of black fly and everyone else's as well! While Mother was about her business I would creep out of doors to the outhouses at the side, for there I knew I could find Mrs. Amies' goose. This certain outhouse had a stable door, the sort that would open at the top and remain closed at the bottom and over this lower half I was able to peer inside. For quite a while we entertained one another, the goose and I. I would hiss to provoke her and she would stretch her long neck, roll her head over sideways to flash her glassy eye and deliver a long string of abuse at me. This conversation piece must have hurt her deeply for when I met her out in the pasture she would make a headlong dive in my direction. With wings flapping and webbed feet running as fast as they could, she would stretch forward her neck to its fullest extent expecting her beak to reach me minutes before the rest of her body. It was such a terrifying sight, that open beak with a long, rolled tongue emerging from the throat to the accompaniment of such violent hissing that I didn't wait to reply and scooted away as fast as my legs would remove me from the scene before everyone came scurrying to see what all the fuss was about.

It was different when I called to play with my friends for then I would go round to the back of the house which fronted the road. Here was a very small courtyard separated from the road by a low wall and here we would sit for hours exchanging our gossip. This wall met the building by a flight of stone steps with no hand-rail to prevent unbalanced athletes from toppling to their doom below but, undaunted by this prospect, we ran up and down these steps as if on a training run. It was the nearest we ever got to the hay loft on the other side of the door where the steps stopped abruptly.

Mrs. Amies' house showing the steps up to the door

We must have created quite a disturbance for on the other side of this narrow road was a white, tubular steel, five-barred gate over which at intervals peered The General! This opposite corner was occupied by Maes Court and its grounds. Maes Court was originally called "The Jewkes," which was how Jewkes Lane got its name. The house was long and low and gracious, as befits a country squire. His gardens were beautifully laid out with rose beds and trellises set amid the grassy paths. We knew all this because in winter when the trees were bare we could peer through the hedges at such a wondrous sight, so different from our cottage garden where I could find so many interesting bits and pieces. The white gate led down a Tarmac drive to the rear entrance and it was always in this region where the General's head would appear, bald and bespectacled, wondering what on earth we could achieve by such a performance. Outside his domain he was a different character altogether, outstanding in his immaculate khaki uniform, leather-gloved hands adjusting his baton beneath his arm and cap set firmly above his moustache - there seemed to be nothing in between! Actually, we were fortunate to catch sight of him at all for, since he was often away on duty when his Lady would also vacate the house, to most of the country folk he was just a myth. We always knew when he was due to return home for Mrs. Amies went over to the house to help the housekeeper give an extra polish to everything so that it sparkled and shone when the owners returned. His Lady I remember as a straight-backed, long-skirted lady with grey hair drawn behind into a tight bun and she only ever performed one activity: she walked along the roads knitting socks!

Maes Court

Betty and I struck up a friendship which was to land us in trouble. We were always on the lookout for something new to do and cooking must have appealed to us but no-one would ever let us experiment on our own. So it was agreed that I would "smuggle" some matches and Betty would "acquire" some candles. This would give us the heat, so we imagined. But what to cook? My sister was with us and so was Michael, who was older than Elizabeth and had a wry neck. He was Mrs. Amies' grand-nephew and was staying with her for a spell. The four of us stood in Betty's hideout (the shed in the orchard) thinking hard. I had seen my mother put lard into the frying pan and as the candle wax melted and dripped it appeared to be just like lard. There was our answer. If we dripped the wax onto a tin lid and heated it over the candle we would have fat in which to cook! What a wonderful idea. There was no limit to our resourcefulness - only the grown ups! They now appeared out of the blue. They had been searching everywhere for us and before they had time to realise what we were up to we hastily covered our tracks, dousing the candles and vigorously wafting the air with our arms before emerging smiling so innocently.

Another of my "resourceful" ideas came because my father smoked and, as cigarettes were bought when available, he had built up quite a stock in the sideboard cupboard, about ten packets of twenty Players Navy Cut! I had noticed these for they looked so attractive standing piled one upon the other, all square, in their cellophane coverings. Having watched my father smoke I wondered what it would be like to try one, so I unobtrusively removed a packet from the cupboard. But when my mother challenged me with the accusation that I had taken a packet I was horrified. Day after day the interrogation took place: "Why did you do it?" queried Mother worriedly.

"But Mummy, I didn't." was my earnest reply.

"What made you do it?" she continued as though she hadn't heard my denial.

"But Mummy, I haven't." I had already discovered that by looking someone straight in the eye unflinchingly I could convince them of my sincerity. So, with hands behind my back, standing straight as a die, I returned stare for stare. Undaunted, she continued questioning "Who asked you to do it?" and undaunted, I replied:

"Why, no-one of course." So it went on.

"God punishes little girls who tell lies, you know. He puts a black mark against their names and He never forgets." (Oh, how I knew that. I had one already for treading on the gravestone in the church!) "God sees everything, nothing escapes His notice. God knows." I was beginning to wonder where I would meet Him. She tried a different approach.

"Whatever wrong has been done, you know, God will forgive if the wrong-doer owns up. There is no need to worry. He forgives all our sins." I remained silent, just listening. We were standing in the outside toilet. Beside me was little Elizabeth, my sister, taking in every word, her large round eyes glancing up first at one face then at the other, first at the interrogator, then the accused. Nothing was said. Mother tried another course.

"You will tell me, Elizabeth, won't you, if she's telling the truth?" and Elizabeth wagged her head solemnly up and down as she gravely replied: "Yes, Mummy."

"And did she take the cigarettes?" This time, just as solemnly she shook her head from side to side clearly answering: "No, Mummy."

Well, that was that! Elizabeth couldn't be lying. And my face was so innocent I must be telling the truth. She shook her head in dismay. Next time Mother called at Mrs. Amies' the situation was discussed again. "She must have done. They must have been stolen from your house. We've none here. Betty has no access to such things."

"Well, if they'd had them they would have made themselves sick! Smoking a whole packet of cigarettes would have made them as sick as pigs and would have turned their faces green!" My face certainly wasn't green, neither had I been in the least bit poorly.

"You must be mistaken," stated Mrs. Amies with determination.

"I tell you, I'm not," replied Mother and with such a deadlock situation between them she and Mrs. Amies parted company rather sourly.

Day after day passed by with more questions asked and more hints dropped. Someone would crack. Elizabeth couldn't hold out if she knew anything because a five-year-old could be so easily tricked into giving the game away. But at last it was me who surrendered. How was I to know that Mr. Went, the road man, had stood on the other side of the hedge, boggling at the sight before his eyes. (Mr. Went's job as road man was to see that all roadside ditches in his patch were kept clear of debris, thus preventing flooding of fields after heavy rain or melting snow. He also repaired the paths.) There was Betty and Michael and that girl from the cottage, along with her little blond-haired sister, sitting with their backs against the back of an old shed wall thinking they were unobserved. There they sat, all in a row, knees hunched up before them in the confined space, all smoking cigarettes one after another, red glowing from the tips and smoke drifting upwards through the leaves. A comical sight it was, but for the seriousness of it. These children were far too young to be smoking. I was nine and Elizabeth was five. It was unheard of. They would be ill. But apart from that they might set fire to the shed. He must have stood and watched till we departed from the scene, unaware that there had been a witness to our wickedness. We had started off by walking along the lane puffing away at our cigarettes. Elizabeth and Michael were too young to expect a whole one each. We had cut theirs in half! We had to be on our guard for at the slightest sound we bent down and stubbed them out on the road, continuing to walk along with the appearance of having not a care in the world. When we felt safe once more we would "light up" again. This became so hazardous that we sought the seclusion of the back of the shed. As for my denials, once having set out upon a course it was very difficult to change direction. I was in very deep water and I knew it. Mother's cure for telling lies was to rub soap over my tongue to clean it and, as I had told so many, this was not a very pleasant prospect! (I laugh now because I tried the same cure on my seven-year-old son and resignedly he stood before me with his tongue out waiting for the treatment. It never occurred to him to protest!) Unknown before now was the fact that this was not my initiation into the habit of smoking!

It came about like this. The headmaster had a daughter, Sheila, who was older than me and chose her friends with fickleness. First, there was fair-haired Janet, the local policeman's daughter, she was of the right breed! Then there was dark-haired Beryl, another native whose only conversation with me concerned finger nails. Hers were so beautifully shaped and pink while mine were square and white. She could never understand how mine grew straight across the top whereas hers were smoothly rounded. She never guessed that, in order to be different and therefore of some consequence, I used to bite them till they were straight and square with corners! These chosen friends would be allowed to play in Sheila's garden during the playtimes and dinner hour while we nondescripts sat in the field on the outside of her garden fence. I would often sit and chat with Margaret Furnough, leaning nonchalantly against this partition, straining my ears in an attempt to eavesdrop on their secrets until Sheila came and kicked the palings at my back telling me to move away from her fence. She didn't have much time for evacuees, even though I now considered myself an established country girl. Then one day my friend, Margaret, was invited into the sacred enclosure and I was left outside, hurt and bewildered, wondering at the reason for my exclusion and the bald statement issued to me: "No, not you. We don't want you in with us!" It was a sad and puzzled daughter who confided in her mother that night. "Don't worry about people like that," she said. "They're not worth another thought." But think about it she did for when I was setting off for school next morning, I was handed a piece of advice which acted like cheese to a mouse. "If she ever asks you to play, hold your head up high and tell her "No, thank you. It is better on this side of the fence!" What audacity that snooty girl with the pigtails (ME), had! But it worked. She pleaded with me to play with her but this didn't come about until we, Sheila, Janet and I, were the only three girls left at school after all the other children had gone home. I had now to wait for my mother who had joined the Womens' Institute.

It was while this meeting was in progress that I was admitted to that exclusive circle of friends of the Headmaster's daughter. I was idling away my time in the playground, kicking the brick ends which the builders had scattered around. They were in the throes of building a kitchen so that in due course the children would be able to have a hot midday meal. The job of cook was to be offered to my mother after its completion, perhaps on the strength of her oatmeal fritters, of which I shall say more later, but this she was to decline. As I kicked the bits and pieces from one foot to the other Sheila and Janet crossed the yard bent on reaching the potting shed in the school garden. This was out of bounds to the pupils and seemed like an allotment on the other side of the hedge, reached only by the headmaster's family through the little wicket gate. I looked longingly after them and they turned to catch my expression unawares. Their hearts softened as they once again risked being snubbed by inviting me to join them and, as I had no-one else with whom to pass the time, I joyfully accepted. Through the gate and along the narrow path we went, entering the shed by the door at the end. Once inside, I realised that I was the unexpected guest and everything had been laid out just for the two of them. Along the side wall, opposite the window, was a long, wide shelf which served as a workbench and here was laid out a knife and several tin lids. Then out of her pocket Sheila brought her collection of cigarette stub ends. She must have been collecting them for days, pocketing any which caught her eye. Carefully she placed them out on the work bench and equally carefully each one was trimmed, the larger ones being cut into two. Warily she eyed the window then she tiptoed back down the path just to make quite sure her father was not intending to visit his shed this afternoon. When assured, she returned to the shed and the session began. A match was struck and she and Janet "lit up". "Here's yours, and I was handed my "smoke".

"I can't smoke," I miserably replied for, as they thought, I wasn't as sophisticated as they were.

"Well, have a go then. It's easy. Do it like this." And they puffed away to prove their superiority. Gingerly I held the stub end to my lips while they lit it, almost singeing my nose in the process, and slowly I puffed away. I didn't dare show my distaste for I would have been thrown out of the company and I was sworn to secrecy as to the goings on that evening in the shed in the headmaster's garden.

During the following weeks an observer would see a smile flicker over my face as I passed by that wicket gate, occasionally glancing through the hedge to make sure the shed was still there and doubtless there were many heads wondering how I'd managed to worm my way in on the other side of the garden fence during play and lunch times but, of course, I was a potential blackmailer. If they didn't keep me close in their grips there was no knowing what whispers might circulate.

Country gatherings were attended by all the women in the vicinity as a means of hearing all the local news and exchanging all the gossip. The gathering that took place on the afternoon of my initiation into smoking was in the form of a Women's Institute meeting. These were held at the school after classes once a month and at each one an activity was suggested for the next. There had been the competition of the supper dish. Each member had to prepare her favourite supper dish at a cost of just a few pence. For three weeks my mother had pored over wartime economy recipe books until at last she found one she liked the look of. Oatmeal fritters. With instructions open before her she carefully measured into the basin a handful of oats and a handful of grated cheese. These were bound together with powdered egg and a little milk and seasoned with salt and pepper. She rolled the dough into balls and patted them flat before frying them to an attractive golden brown. Then with her "favourite supper" fritters placed in a dish in her basket she set off for the meeting. After careful inspection and much prodding and poking the verdict was given. This member had made the favourite supper dish so attractive. It smelled so appetising and was so cheap to prepare. Would anyone care to sample it? All hands stretched forward and soon the fritters had disappeared. They were pronounced delicious. As Mother said afterwards, she was a fraud! "Favourite Supper Dish" indeed, when she had never made it before and, as for that, she had no notion of what it tasted like! But she won. However, I never remember her cooking them again. Whenever Mother cooked I always helped, especially greasing the tins or pans. We used the wrappers from the butter, margarine or lard which had been scraped of every vestige of fat, leaving only a glossy smear. This had to be rubbed over the pan and whenever I asked for a tiny little bit more I'm afraid I was turned down, as more could not be spared. I just had to rub harder!

Then there was the night of the whist drive which replaced a W.I. meeting. Mother went for the news and gossip as usual, but she hadn't a clue how to play whist and hated any game of cards. So, as the tables were made up, she sat like a wallflower against the wall. "We are one short. Will you take this chair?" They were all looking in her direction. Growing terribly flustered with all this attention her words tumbled out one after the other: "Oh, I'm sorry, I can't play whist. I can't play cards at all. I hate cards. Oh, I'm so sorry, I couldn't." There were mumbles from all tables as heads were bent in consultation. Then all heads raised and there was silence. The Chairwoman spoke: "Couldn't you possibly help us out and join in, for if you don't three others will have to drop out?"

Hastily considering her ungracious refusal, she hesitated just long enough for the Chairwoman to add "We'll all help you as you go along," and turning to the rest of the company with an inarguable "Won't we?" they all nodded their heads in assent and Mother was led to the chair. She found herself sitting opposite the best and most revered player of the gathering. Having been told that if she couldn't follow suit, she should trump the cards, she proceeded to do just this TO ALL HER PARTNER'S CARDS! She was delighted! At the end of the evening the time came for the winner to be announced and, taking little notice of the names called out, she was surprised to find her own name being called. She had won a prize. Well, fancy that! Admittedly it was the booby prize but to win something at all gave pleasure. "And the booby prize is a hundredweight of swedes." Mother was astounded. A hundredweight of swedes! What on earth was she going to do with a hundredweight of swedes? She didn't even like them enough to eat more than a little slice when she had no apples and, as for cooking them they made her feel sick! I do believe she forgot about them on purpose – until the next W.I. meeting, that is, for it was then that the announcement brought her face to face with her problem. "Would the winner of the hundredweight of Swedes from the last meeting please collect them for they are rotting in the corner of my field." Heavens above! Never would she be induced to play whist again. In desperation she gave them away to our nearest neighbour who lived outside the orchard – a family which intrigued me no end – providing of course that they would collect them. They were pleased with the gift. Mother had some for us too and on many evenings following, while sitting by the fire listening to the programmes on the wireless, we could be heard crunching away on a chunk of swede, which Mother had cut and peeled like an apple.

Another month's activity was the re-creation of a garment, something new from something old. The re-made garment was a great success for with this she won second prize, although the general consensus of opinion was that it was the first one she should have been awarded. My father had worn out his best brown and white striped shirt and, with great patience; Mother had unpicked it all and re-cut the freshly laundered pieces. The back cut out the back, the fronts the front and the sleeves produced just enough good material for the sleeves, all for a tailored, long-sleeved blouse for me. Material could not be bought for love nor money so this was an outstanding exhibit. It fitted perfectly and I looked so smart in it. I was certainly a tailor-made sort of child. Indeed, this was the title I had been given when accompanying my sister to the hospital some years earlier for her massage and remedial exercises. "Here comes Miss Tailor-Made" was the nurse's greeting on our arrival. I was no beauty, not like Elizabeth. She was always a target for comment with her platinum-blonde hair falling in pageboy style on to her shoulders. It waved gently, beautifully, from a side parting and was caught back out of her eyes with the largest, prettiest, widest piece of hair ribbon which could be bought. These bows always reminded me of huge exotic butterflies which had delicately alighted on the top of a mound of gold. I had plaits! - long, straight, brown ones, with small, dark, neat ribbons at their ends and my face was smothered in freckles. Just to stress these features I generally wore a beret tugged smartly over one ear. The only points in common between us were our eyes, for I could point out truthfully "My eyes are like Elizabeth's". Blue!

CHAPTER VIII

Elizabeth was now allowed to go to school if she felt like it! She had reached the required age, but although she longed to go with her "big sister", Mother wondered if she really was strong enough. It was such a long journey too. After discussion with the Headmaster it was agreed that she should begin attendance and, as it was such a distance to school, I could push her there in the pram. So it was that alongside all the bicycles in the school yard I would park THE PRAM! What sniggers were directed at me; but there was nothing to be done about it. I was in charge of my sister and I carried that responsibility with pride. We would set off at the usual time with Elizabeth sitting on newspapers we had saved for the war effort and which would be stacked in the school cloakroom awaiting collection. Only if the weather was fine would we go via Jewkes Lane. Even then I would have great difficulty pushing the pram up the steep slope of Church Hill. I remember telling Elizabeth she would have to get out and push as I could not manage it by myself!

Most times we took the longer route which joined up with the Long Length   because this was far more level. Although it was longer it was selected for the ease it offered and through this change in the journey I made several new friends.

Elma came from the New Inn, half way along the road that led to the Long Length. She would often lend a hand in pushing and with the extra help we would arrive at school earlier than usual. On wet days we would be barred from using the field for play but during the hot summer days the gate into Robin Hood (as the field was known) would be wide open as an indication that we could leave the playground behind and be as free as the wind amongst the grasses.

Robin Hood was large and from its height we could see over the cluster of houses between the trees that bordered the main road to Tenbury. The field was on the same level as the playground, along the side of it and across the top as far as the headmaster's garden where I had sat on my side of the fence! But then from this height it sloped steeply for a quarter of a mile till it reached the same level as the main road where it flattened out again before reaching the trees. Down at the left-hand corner, at the bottom of the slope, was a brook but we never went as far as this. We hardly ever reached the bottom of the slope because, like all other children, we would lose track of the time and when the bell was rung from the top of the hill to summon us to afternoon lessons we would have to huff and puff up that slope as fast as we could using mole hills and tufts of grass as footholds so as not to be late for the marking of the register. It behoved us to set our sights no further than half way down and it was here where we would often sit eating dandelion leaves. It was not that we were hungry or under-nourished, it was just the craze. After all, rabbits ate dandelion leaves and some of the farmers' wives made delicious dandelion wine so why not try them ourselves?

It was my time of torment. On this occasion I had remained in the playground. The morning break was fairly short and several of us were standing chatting in the playground instead of going further away from school into the field when, out of the corner of my eye, I saw a disturbance up by the gate. Some of the boys were having fun. Then I noticed, to my horror, that they were pushing and bouncing my pram along Robin Hood, having a grand old time. One would pull the handle this way and another that way and it zig-zagged it's bouncing path right before my eyes. But I was in the playground and in order to get to it I would have to go up the yard to the gate then down the other side of the fence on the field side. But I could not stand up to that group of boys. They were so much older and bigger than me. Some of them were almost fourteen for this school taught the children from the beginning to the end of their school life. That pram was no lightweight folder but the kind with springs underneath and a foot portion which could be lowered in order to accommodate the growing child. It was a well-built baby perambulator and the only means of transporting my sister home. She could never walk the distance.

With shrieks of laughter and many glances in my direction to see how I was reacting, the boys urged the pram further and further towards the top of the slope and just as it went over the ridge and began to disappear they hared back to the safety of the playground.

Gradually gathering momentum, the pram bounced and rebounded until at last it overturned and somersaulted to the bottom of the hill where it came to rest upside down with the handle in the mud of the brook. With tears streaming down my face I could think of nothing but recovering it and therefore followed its course, gathering speed myself, till I too was dangerously close to losing my balance. As I reached it and struggled to set it to rights, the distant ringing of the school bell reached my ears and so there was I, all alone at the very bottom of Robin Hood, about to struggle up the slope with the pram. Fortunately, it was intact although how it remained so was unbelievable. By "tacking" upwards and alternately pulling and pushing it over the hummocks I was able eventually to return it to the playground and then myself to the classroom, with great sobs escaping from my lips and tears of distress from my eyes. I hated those boys and, after what the Headmaster must have said to them, that sentiment was returned and for a time, until they felt revenge had been taken, they made my life a misery.

I could not return home along the Long Length as I had to collect the milk. These days the empty can remained with me throughout my school hours, sometimes in my desk or my lunch bag, sometimes carefully concealed under my coat on the peg in the cloakroom. It varied in order to confuse the would-be thieves.

As the infants finished lessons earlier than the juniors, Elizabeth had to come into our classroom for the last half hour of the day's schooling and she would sit in my desk squashed between me and whoever happened to be sitting next to me. This was also the arrangement at dinnertime for I always took the sandwiches for the two of us to save her bothering about them and she would come and eat her dinner with me – that is if there was any left, for it happened one day that someone had been hunting around and had taken a fancy to the food in my desk so that when Elizabeth joined me feeling ravenously hungry I could find nothing to give her except two plain biscuits which had obviously not appealed to the thief. Poor Elizabeth went hungry that day, like me, but we survived.

The boys now took it into their heads to follow a new sport. The hedges along Jewkes Lane afforded excellent cover for them as they lay in wait for any girls whose misfortune it was to pass along that road. They chose this spot with the knowledge that just a little further along there was a field prolific in the growth of giant thistles.

All the girls having to travel that route, including myself with Elizabeth and the pram, would wait for each other at the end of afternoon school in the mistaken belief that there was safety in numbers, but the closer we got to the fearful spot the less safe we felt. As we crept along the road hoping to escape the boys' notice they would suddenly rush out at us trying to grab anyone who was not fast enough to elude their grasp. This was when the pram came in useful since we could use it as a battering ram, having first let my sister climb out. Fortunately, the boys were not interested in her and she would pass by unscathed.

There was worse trouble in store for us, though, when I did not have the pram, either because Elizabeth had not come to school or because she had felt able to do without it. On these days we all mustered at the crossroads and at the count of "three" would try to rush the area, arms linked and spreading ourselves across the entire road. We did vainly hope this fearsome sight would prove too much for our captors but there was no such luck. When one unfortunate female was caught the rest knew they were relatively free from further harassment and were compelled to stand aside and watch, unable to help the victim as she would be carried unceremoniously to the largest patch of thistles and be dumped therein. The experience was painful but then boys are unfeeling creatures and delight in the torture of lesser mortals.

      There were afternoons when I tried a different strategy. Elizabeth was now old enough to go home by herself and left school half-an-hour earlier than I, so I was able to go faster by myself and would try to get out ahead of everyone else. As soon as the bell was rung for the end of the afternoon I would move as though a demon were chasing me. Slinging on my outdoor clothes I would tear down the path, through the gate, and race along the road to Church Hill. Going in this direction was no problem, for the slithery downward gradient was a help to a maid fleeing from her captors. Past Adams' I would go, not even glancing around or noticing whether there were cows in the vicinity, gradually reducing my speed, for my legs were beginning to tremble. Turning round to see how much leeway there was I would be relieved to find myself alone so, slowing to a quick walk past the rectory, I would appear through Mrs. Amies' back door breathless and in haste. I could not state my reason for such a hurry but she must have been in sympathy because she too now began to bustle, confusing me as well as herself into the bargain. Once handed the full can of milk I would hastily throw my thanks to the wind in her direction and rush forward to attack Jewkes Lane. If I were lucky I would clear it before the boys had realised they had missed the boat. But should I prove to be unlucky I was to rue every minute spent in carrying out my errand. With eyes searching from right to left I would go as quietly as I could in haste and having almost reached the pool, feeling more safe in the knowledge that there were less places in which to hide after this, I would suddenly be bounded upon with blood-curdling yells and flailing arms. They would try to take away my milk can. That was the reason for the wire handle being such a peculiar shape. They would tug my plaits and call me horrible names. As fast as I would run to escape they would out stride me and trip me up, threatening me with the thistle treatment. Yet I must not show them how really frightened I was. If only they had guessed how near to breaking down I had been perhaps they would have given up much sooner. Those days when Mother took it into her head to walk along the road to meet me were Heaven sent. I confided some of my fears to her and received a certain degree of comfort. "You must walk along with your head held high," (I always had to hold my head high but it got me into such dreadful situations!) "and tell them "Bricks and stones may break my bones but names can never hurt me!" The boys became so sick of my singing this song that they would repeat it over and over again in varying funny voices, all to add to my distress. Of the five or six boys involved I did wish George would not join in. He was the nicest looking and usually so well mannered. I rather liked George. Strange how even nice boys turned nasty in the company of lesser desirables.

But time progresses and old activities give way to new and I suppose the boys thought they had taken their revenge by now. I must, by this time, have been ten years old. These hostilities were forgotten and I found myself in the company of George down in the copse. Below the meadow bordering the cherry orchard in which ABC was situated was a small patch of trees through which ran a twisting, bubbling brook. The ground around was boggy but higher up on the other side it dried out beneath the pine trees. Down by the brook grew the most beautiful king-cups. Certainly they were king-size marsh marigolds. Their stems were so thick and strong looking, supporting the deep golden heads like miniature saucers. I could not refrain from picking a bunch, although it meant squelching through the bog, whenever I strayed in this direction which became more and more frequent. Any marsh marigolds I have since discovered have disappointed me terribly. They would only be described as overgrown buttercups. A thought has occurred to me: why did everything seem so beautiful, so much larger than life? Was it really because I myself was smaller? Was I experiencing the same feelings as Alice when she was in Wonderland? For, looking back, this was my wonderland.

Past this copse were two houses, side by side but end on to the road, and a little pathway ran along beside the pine trees leading first to Derek's house and then to George's. Derek had his cousin Della living with him and George's mother had taken an evacuee, Doreen Bingham, and due to the proximity of the copse to their houses it was their natural playground; trees to climb, the brook to paddle in and what a place for hide and seek. But when I was asked to join them during the long summer evenings I brought my own brand of play with me.

Maybe because I had been in the hospital so frequently, I had more idea of the diverse activities carried out there. I had been asked to practise remedial exercises alongside Elizabeth and so encourage her, and well I remember walking a straight line along the hospital carpet with my toes curled round treading only on the outside of my feet, or picking up marbles with my toes and transferring them from the floor to a container.

Elizabeth was encouraged to do better than me and so correct and strengthen her limbs. For hours I had watched the bandages being wrapped around splints by both the nurses in the hospital and my mother at home. It was natural, therefore, for me to bring this knowledge into play. For hours we were doctors, nurses and patients. George was the oldest. He wore spectacles and was the most natural choice for the doctor. Doreen, who lived at his house, obviously had more contact with him and was always chosen to be his nurse. This left the other three of us to be their patients. I ran down to this new hospital armed with pieces of wood and rag which could be torn into strips and sat among the pine needles to await the arrival of the staff! In due course Doctor George would attend to my wounds and Nurse Doreen would give me my medicine and then I would be told to lie and rest. The warm sunshine and sweet-smelling pines were conducive to the welfare of any would-be convalescent and I would stay there resting while the others were being attended to. As I progressed I could hobble on makeshift crutches. These were suitable branches which I had been able to fetch when I realised these were what I needed. Off I would run, legs all bandaged, quite oblivious of the fact that I was in terrible pain from my "wounds" and, having found the suitably-shaped crutches, I would hurry back with them. After displaying them with pride I would proceed to hobble hither and thither, visiting less mobile cripples. This arrangement was continual and my enthusiasm as a patient began to wane. I did so wish I could be George's nurse. Doreen was constantly at his side while I was treated with such indifference but whenever I suggested a change I was reminded to be a good patient and keep quiet. Oh dear, could I never be George's constant companion?

A short while after this my fortunes changed. My hopes rose. Seated in the cottage window one Saturday afternoon, looking out, who should I see walking beneath the trees but George himself. He opened the gate, walked up the path and knocked hesitantly on our front door. My mother and I answered it together. "Could Ann come with us tonight? Father's taking us into town to the pictures to see 'The Wizard of Oz'." Oh, I was beside myself with joy. I would love to go. And so it came about that I went to the cinema for the very first time in my life. Later that afternoon the family arrived in their car and I was ushered into the back where George and the other children were squashed. After a swinging, bouncing ride over the country roads we found ourselves sitting, quite a while later, in the darkness of the stalls watching the much discussed film. I was as frightened as could be when the Witch appeared during a hurricane and I wept bitterly when she took away a small black Scottie dog in her bicycle basket. How cruel and wicked she was. This touched on my previous history for I had had a black Scottie of my own who had been run over by a car and, to me, this dog in the film was my own Sally.

It was late at night when George's Father returned me to the welcome safety of the cottage but, after an evening of elation mixed with fear, my experience during that film stayed with me and was intensified when I first caught sight of Peg. Here was the witch of the film in person. She lived on the opposite side of the road to George in a tumble-down cottage, barely visible through the trees. We knew she was reputed to live there but it was months before she appeared to us in the flesh. All villages and hamlets are supposed to have an eccentric and, to us children, here she was. We were all afraid of her. She was thin and upright in stature and, as with all witches, was dressed from head to toe in black. At least, I assume her lower regions were draped in black. We could only guess for our eyes never saw anything below her waist. She neither saw nor heard us for we stood silently at the roadside in awe of the figure sitting perched high up in her trap holding the reins taut before her as her horse daintily trotted his way along the road drawing her stately form behind him. She turned into her cart track and disappeared into oblivion and, although we often poked our noses through the hedge or jumped to peer over the top, we never saw her pottering around her cottage or appearing in any other guise at all. We did smell smoke and saw it rising above her trees and, if we had gone up the hill behind her cottage, we would have seen her bonfire blazing away at all hours of the day and well into the evening. The glow worried us a great deal because we were conscious of the need for blackout so as not to attract the attention of the enemy planes which might easily pass over our part of the country. But I suppose Peg did not have a newspaper and doubt if she knew what a wireless was. Therefore, she carried on in her own weird way, not knowing that there was a war at all. We did not enlighten her. We did not interfere. Witches were safe if left to their own devices and we had no desire to upset the present community.

As for George, we seemed to travel our different paths after this, for the time came for him to leave school and start work so it was with great surprise that I was to see him several years later. I was sitting on the "long seat" of a Birmingham Corporation bus watching the passengers alight when, down the stairs, came a young man who seemed vaguely familiar. The spectacles, the face, who was it? I remained unnoticed, an habitual occurrence, but followed his every movement whilst delving into the depths of my mind. As he left the platform of the bus, too late for any introductions or reminiscences, I knew who he was – George. For a long time I wondered what he was doing in this part of the country. I was not mistaken over his identity, I was certain, although we are all said to have doubles, but my wondering was soon satisfied for the Birmingham Evening Mail displayed an announcement in the engagements column – George Randle to Doreen Bingham. I was really very happy for them.

RANDLE—BINGHAM.—The engagement is announced between George William, only child of Mr. and Mrs. Randle, of Knighton-on-Teme, and Doreen Emily, only child of Mr. and Mrs. Bingham, of Alum Rock.

The Engagement Announcement.

The hill rising up behind Peg's property was known as Abraham's Bosom but, as youngsters, this was too delicate a name for us to use so we called it Pigeon Hill. Over the top and way down the dip lived the Guys, two boys who were older than me and in the top class, the headmaster's class. I remember them well for they were the only boys who managed to smile when I met them. I felt they were friends. In fine weather this walk over Pigeon Hill was a quick way to Davis's farm, the distance as defined by one side of a square you might say. But in bad weather it was a tramp along the roads ending with a squelch through the mud up the rutted cart track. It was at Davis's that my father's cousin had installed his wife and daughter. Uncle Howard, as he was to us, had heard how much we were enjoying our sojourn in the country away from the worries of the war and felt it a safe place in which to deposit his wife, our Aunt Miriam, and their daughter, Carol, just about twelve months old, but Aunt Miriam did not share our experiences or delights. It just was not her cup of tea. To begin with she had shingles, such a painful complaint for which little treatment can be given and with a small daughter so utterly dependent on her she had to grin and bear it. Then Carol caught whooping cough with such a degree of severity that my Aunt was worried to death and complained bitterly about the isolation she suffered there. She felt so alone when she needed company so much. Our two families were rather strangers to each other in those days and our contacts were infrequent. I am glad to know that much closer fellowship came to pass with the years. I mention this Aunt's arrival because Uncle Howard also came down at weekends and many are the times that he and my father were destined to make the journey together.

Elizabeth and me in the orchard

Auntie Cis and Mother at the cottage gate

Mother in the lane by the New Inn

Auntie Cis, Elizabeth and me in the orchard

Elizabeth wearing her leather collar

There are delights round every bend if one knows where to look and Tom became my shining light for a time. He was about twenty but, as with all country lads, he looked much younger, or would have done if I had been able to see his face beneath a week's growth of hair. Tom was the youngest son of the farmer who owned our cottage and was therefore often to be found in and around the orchard. As he walked past our gate I would step out alongside him in order to find out where he was going. His attire was generally quite odd to say the least. Great big boots encased his feet and sacking bound his legs, tied beneath the knees with string. As I generally met him on rainy days I should have expected to find him wearing some kind of waterproof outer garment, but over his breeches and jacket and slung around his neck was another larger sack and over his head – why, yes, the corner of yet another sack. But in spite of his appearance he was kind enough to suffer my company and chatter. We would pass through the gate at the top of the orchard and out into the meadow on to another gate before I would ask: "Where are you heading for today?" Somewhat daunted I would hear his answer:

"Too far for you to come. You had better go back home now."

and so as not to offend him I would stay where I was and watch him stride off into the distance. Some hours later he would return with his sheep which he would park in the orchard, outside our garden fence. That suited me. He would have to come back and collect them before long.

On one of his shorter walks, with me as his uninvited companion, he showed me where the mushrooms grew under the hedge, below the trees at the back of beyond. We had known for some time now that there were mushrooms growing in the area for it had been Tom's father who had knocked at our door quite early in the day asking if Mother was interested in buying mushrooms. "Why, yes." She answered somewhat wonderingly for, first of all, it was very unusual for the old man to call on us, or anyone else for that matter, and secondly there was no evidence of the whereabouts of a mushroom salesman. The old man watched Mother's face for several seconds weighing up her answer until she began to feel rather uncomfortable, then from his pocket he withdrew a filthy handkerchief. Carefully unwrapping the four corners he exposed about a dozen mushrooms for which he asked half-a-crown. Since Mother had already shown her agreement to the purchase she duly paid him his asking price and after he had left, pleased with his bargain, she turned slowly inside the house, a weird expression on her face. She just could not bring herself to use those mushrooms, however well she washed them, so that was literally money down the drain! I learned from Tom that these mushrooms had to be collected early in the morning before the sun was up and while the dew was still on the ground. One had to be there early before anyone else could pick them. I wonder if he guessed who trod out at dawn one morning shortly after that with chip basket over her arm, the dew on the long grass soaking her shoes right through, in order to bring back mushrooms for breakfast, before even Tom or his father awakened to the dawn of a new day.

Tom was brave too. As I came home from school one day I noticed a buzzing in one of the cherry trees. Running into the house I called out to my mother: "There's an awful loud buzzing in one of the trees that I came past."
"It sounds as if the bees are swarming," she said and quickly came back with me to see. She was greeted by an amazing sight. It was as though a huge black curtain was hanging from the bough of the tree, a buzzing, moving curtain, yet strangely stationary. Indeed, the bees were

swarming. "We had better tell Tom," she thought aloud, and set off to search for him. When he was found and told he accepted the news with pleasure.

"I beed lookin for them bees all day long," he said. "I hunted all over for that there queen." It seemed so funny to me for a man to hunt for one bee but I learnt that wherever the queen went the swarm of bees followed and wherever she settled that was where the bees would gather. If the queen was caught and returned to the hive the others would find their way back too. In excitement we followed in Tom's footsteps, wondering at his queer apparel. Over his head he had a straw-brimmed hat with fine netting secured right over his face and neck. His hands were covered in thick padded gloves. He was ready for the attack. In silence we watched while he attempted to trap the queen, in turn being attacked from all sides by angry workers. Then a string of abuse was uttered as the queen eluded him and settled in another tree to be followed by her train. The attack began again and at last he achieved his object. With care the queen was returned to her hive outside Tom's father's farm. We were full of admiration for the daring feat but this was not the end of the incident. When news got around that we had discovered a swarm of bees the family from High Point declared they were their bees and they could not be Tom's as he had not any of his own. Then another farmer claimed that they were his since he had lost his a week before and no reports had come to his ears save this one, so they must be his. Of course, everyone joined in, for a hive of bees was valuable to their owner in terms of the honey which they could sell. But how on earth did one identify one's own bees, I wondered? Surely they were not branded like cows or sheep or labelled like cherries. I was mystified.

Our cottage itself was built almost centrally on the plot of land allotted to it. We could walk all round it, admittedly with less room on the left hand side. Here was an outside chimney breast and close to it the upstairs bedroom window which was so low that by standing on the path beneath and reaching upwards one could touch the sill with the finger tips. The positioning of this window explains the commotion which took place in the middle of one night. Mother was disturbed from her sleep by a shuddering noise and, anxious to investigate but fearful of what she might find, she crept to the window. As she opened it something was thrust in from outside and she jumped backwards in fright. When she dared look again in this direction she was utterly amazed to see the cause of the disturbance. A horse had come up to the garden fence and felt like having a good shake and as his head shook he had made this shuddering sound outside the window. As Mother opened it he put his head through while still standing on all fours in the orchard below.

Horses in the orchard.

In the little patch of soil at the side of the chimney breast we had our own private graveyard. We had found a thrush with a broken wing and had tried to nurse it back to health. In a chip basket we had placed a flannel blanket and gently into this we lowered the bird. Having tried to tempt it with milk and morsels of worm, we realised we were too late in our first-aid attempt so, sadly, the bird had to be buried. With all due ceremony and sorrowing hearts we placed him in the hole which we had dug and when the soil was replaced it was planted on top with seed and flower heads found nearby. From then on, whenever we passed this little corner, we bowed our heads in remembrance.

Further round the back of the building was my cook's kitchen. Talk about a witch living down the road, her concoctions would have to be magnificent to better those which I produced. Sawdust pie interlaced with beetroot, turnip and carrot tops, decorated with slices of parsnip and rings of worm; this as a first course to be followed by a dish of mud representing chocolate blancmange stirred around with mildewed damsons and any other ingredient to which my attention was drawn. Drink was a foul-smelling liquid to which rose petals had been added to delight the eye. I spent hours digging and delving amongst the rubbish which inevitably accumulates out of sight at the rear of country cottages.

While I was lost in invention my mother would be sawing away, backwards and forwards, till her arm developed a larger muscle than she thought possible. Occasionally she would disappear indoors and then we secretly tried to saw as she did testing our biceps every few minutes to see if they were developing likewise. Stacked in the yard at the rear were branches and tree trunks in order to dry off before being used as fuel for our fire. A tree trunk was placed upon the wooden frame – a horse, it was called – ready for sawing and Mother would devote her entire afternoon to rendering it log-size to fit the grate. When at last the saw penetrated, the log would drop with a thud onto the pile of sawdust growing below. It was a very rhythmic sound, rather soothing to the nerves and certainly very good exercise. But how those logs would spit and splutter when put on the glowing fire. The sparks shot out with a miniature explosion and the sap from the still wet logs would ooze and froth to the accompaniment of a fascinating hissing song. This fire was our only source of heat apart from the fragile calor-gas cooker in the kitchen and on this fire generally stood a large black kettle in order to have hot water when required. There was no electricity so the fire must always be red enough to heat the flat irons Mother was obliged to use to iron the clothes. This living room was the hub of our indoor activities and the evenings here were delightful.

As soon as dusk approached and it was too dark to see any longer indoors our first course of action was to "put up the blackout". For fear of attracting enemy aircraft not a light was allowed to shine out through windows or doors. Even the slightest chink of light shining through a badly drawn curtain would bring the police force to one's door. Our cottage window was large and if only it had extended another foot to the floor we would have had French doors instead of the window. Blackout material – a thick twill-like material dyed black – was usually purchased for curtains but our full-length green velvet ones from home were found to be equally effective and provided ample coverage. Just to be on the safe side, however, we had a heavy wooden "shutter" to manoeuvre as well. Father was taking no chances and so he had used half of our table-tennis table, strengthened with battens originally positioned to secure this table-tennis board over our dining room table and now providing a ledge by which we could lift this heavy piece of wood into position over the window. Great effort was involved as only Father could lift it alone and, as he was generally not with us, it required the combined strength of my mother and me. Once the shutter was in position, the latches firmly in place and the curtains drawn across it we were secure for the night.

Next on the list was the lighting of the two paraffin lamps. One had an all-brass base and the other a beautiful red glass container for the paraffin through which we could see the soggy wick. The knobs were turned to raise the two wicks in each lamp – they had been lowered the night before to extinguish the light – and a match was struck to light them. Ah, light at last! But we had first made sure there was enough paraffin in each base for the evening. That was a chore in itself, filling the lamps each day and cleaning the wicks as well. Uncleaned wicks meant smoking lamps and this oversight left the tell-tale black smoke circles on the ceiling. Forgetting to fill the lamps meant a spell of darkness while we would fumble around for the funnel and can of paraffin trying frantically to remember where we last put them. But when all was well, it was a very cosy room.

We had favourite radio programmes for each night of the week, "Monday Night at Eight", "Itma", and so on, which we were allowed to listen to before going up to bed. I well remember the evening my father was expected to come and I waited up for him to arrive, then the cosiness of sitting with him in the giant winged armchair while we listened to a programme usually outside my sphere. Unlike the children of today, our imaginations were exercised to the full and our ears strained to catch every word. There was no television for us. Another evening I remember sitting snug in the same armchair with my grandmother whilst she read me a story.

So this cosy setting was a magnet for all friends and relatives, however distant they may have been. It was a haven of refuge from the turmoil of war as it was experienced back home in the city. For weekends, for weeks, and for holidays too, there was a never-ending stream of visitors to our house. Some enjoyed the peace and quiet, others came out of curiosity, and for some it was an event never to be repeated. Irene was the niece of my mother's life-long friend and she suffered more than most. Poor Irene! She stood about five feet eleven, her head almost touching our rather low ceilings whenever she tried to move. Unfortunately she was slow to realise that in country properties many ceilings are supported by beams and all doors have lintels and so it was inevitable that every time she moved about the cottage her head struck one or more of the beams. We fell to shouting "Mind your head," the moment she showed signs of leaving her seat, partly to protect her head and mostly to save us rendering more first aid. She also had the misfortune to attract a wasp while in the middle of Sunday lunch. Now Irene and wasps had a hatred of each other, a hatred which developed on sight, and such a scene and commotion had I never witnessed before nor, thankfully, since. She screamed as if being murdered and tried to scramble her way over legs to leave the room as quickly as possible, arms flailing and her head ducking this way and that. We tried to calm her but by now she was hysterical and, in an effort to rid the room of the insect, we had all armed ourselves with rolled up papers trying desperately to swat the wasp but managing only to land swipes on each other. While Irene was crying with fear we were laughing till the tears ran down our cheeks. Irene departed before her allotted time, never to return.

Dorothy was altogether different. She paid us innumerable visits and we enjoyed the time she devoted to us two children. She had dark hair deeply waved and I always studied those waves with envy till at last she agreed to help me to achieve the same effect. No setting lotion or curlers were at our disposal, but honest-to-goodness water. She loosened my plaits while I stood before the bedroom window, the ewer on the table full of water. Then she would dip the comb in the water and drag it through my hair until my head was soaking wet. I might just as well have put my head in the jug and saved time! Then by pinching my hair between her first and second fingers and pushing my head into the middle of next week she formed such beautiful deep waves I was afraid to move. They were secured with hundreds of grips, or so it seemed, and there I stood encased in ironmongery with the wind blowing through the window till my head had dried out. It was worth it! I was on the way to being beautiful, which is all a young girl ever wants to be. By the next morning I was back in plaits but anxiously awaiting the next beautifying session.

These hairdressing sessions were so different to my mother's. For her we sat on a stool in the kitchen beside a bowl of paraffin and in her hand she wielded a fine-toothed comb. Regularly we succumbed to this treatment, for head lice were very much in evidence down at school. There was only the one known remedy. Mother would dip the comb in the bowl of paraffin then, beginning at the parting, she would drag the comb right down to the ends of our hair, scraping the very roots as she went. Woe betide us if a knot should impede the progress. Again and again, advancing the width of the comb with each stroke, she would travel round our heads till we reeked with vapour, and had a match been struck we would have gone up in flames. Satisfied that we were "clean", we would then suffer a shampoo, our scalps being massaged thoroughly to ensure that this time the smell of paraffin was completely removed instead of the suspected nits and lice. My goodness, we knew we were clean when she had finished, she left herself and us in no doubt. I suppose other parents were not so thorough for the nurse was often in school peering through the hairs on our heads; so often in fact that it became a game with us, mimics as children are.

Looking back at this time I realise in my innocence and curiosity that I was rather rude and hurtful as my comments were directed at one unfortunate girl. I drew my friend Betty into my confidence. Sometime after I had left her Mrs. Bourne had taken into her care a girl from a Home and this girl always came to school in a red woolly pixie hood but she never removed it. This strange behaviour gave us reason for speculation as we tried to discover why. She would not tell us, but we noticed that she had no hair showing beneath. Whenever she went to the toilet it was always alone whereas we always went in with our friends. It puzzled me. All the girls I knew had long hair. It was the fashion then, as now, and all the boys were cropped very short. I confided my thoughts to Betty: "You don't think she is really a boy dressed as a girl, do you?" Little did I realise then that country confidences become village gossip and how hard I learned my lesson. My thoughts reached Mrs. Bourne in less time than it takes to tell and I was said to be a cruel, unkind, thoughtless, naughty little girl. Mrs. Bourne said that! Mrs. Bourne who had been so kind to me, whom I had grown to respect and love. Is that how she thought I had turned out now that I had left her care and gone to live with my mother? It was a slight on my upbringing, a slight on my mother's code of living. Never again was I to whisper my thoughts to a soul. I would store them all and ponder over them alone when I was safely in my bed. The girl in question had unfortunately been so badly infested with nits and lice that they had been the initial cause of the development of impetigo and, in order to clear up this distressing condition, she had had to have all her hair shaved off. Impetigo was cleared after the continual application of a brilliantly coloured purple ointment and, in order to conceal this fact, our comrade was allowed to wear her hood until her hair grew again.

How she must have suffered – far more than I did, yet I was the reason for added unhappiness. I do hope she forgave me in time.

Anyone with impetigo shone out like a beacon for the purple ointment was certainly an eye-catcher. How distressing it must have been walking round advertising the fact that you were afflicted. Mind you, we nearly all suffered from something or other, it was the fashion; like a lot of old women we all had to be able to talk about "my complaint". Fortunately, my own complaint was much less visible. It affected me between the fingers where the skin would itch like mad and I would be obliged to scratch until it either blistered or bled. No cream or ointment would relieve it so Mother marched me off to the doctor's. After examination and consideration, he pronounced scabies. "How on earth would she get that, Doctor?" asked Mother. "None of us has ever had it."

"No, but unless you are very careful you will! It is a highly contagious disease."

Oh dear, Mother was always so thorough in her efforts at cleanliness. Where had she slipped up? "Where on earth has it come from?" she queried.

"Does she climb over gates and stiles?" enquired the doctor.

"Try to stop her!" said Mother who never knew whether she would find me the right way up or upside down. It was quite the joke just then that if you saw a body walking on hands, feet waving in the air, or parked against a tree upside down, there would be no need to look twice to guess who. It was me! It stands to reason then that if a piece of wood appeared before me I would either climb over it or jump over it, cartwheel or vault over it, sideways, longways or highways! It never occurred to me to step around it or pass through it if it was a gate. Thus whenever I put my hands on the top bar of a stile or gate I was in danger of picking up a little mite transmitted there from the cows who continually rubbed themselves against such obstacles. This mite would then contrive to burrow under the skin and cause the irritation from which I was now suffering. It took weeks to clear it up but at least I did not have a purple ointment to stress the fact.

Me upside down with Elizabeth and Margaret Gaunt, another friend.

For the duration of a visitor's stay the bedroom at the top of the stairs was set aside for their use and Elizabeth and I each had our beds in Mother's room, there being plenty of space to accommodate us all and although healthily tired from the day's activities, the long walks to and from school and fresh air to fill my lungs umpteen times over, I was never tired for sleep. I spent hours with my thoughts. I would amuse myself in the twilight watching the patterns which the leaves of the trees outside the window made on the ceiling above me. By continually staring at them for long periods it must have had an effect on my pupils or even the retina of my eye, for strange things began to happen. I could look at an object stacked on top of the wardrobe and it would appear gigantic, out of all proportion, and, as I continued to stare at it, the object would gradually grow smaller and smaller and smaller, as though seen through a telescope with the wrong end placed to the eye. I tried the game on Panda, which sat on the box against the wall, and to my satisfaction Panda also grew and disappeared and I could actually view the whole scene again while looking at the empty ceiling. How peculiar it all was. Tiring at last of this occupation I imagined shadows turning into people, some pleasant, most of them gruesome, and so obsessed did I become with my imaginary company that I was fearful of my safety and sanity to the extent that I would shoot down to the bottom of the bed under the sheets in order to escape. As nothing happened I gradually eased my way towards the pillow and, with eyes screwed up tight save for one little peephole, I would timidly look to see if they were still there – the people I mean, not the shadows! But the crunch came shortly after Christmas. Elizabeth had had a new teddy bear and Mother had dressed my doll in a beautiful new set of clothes. She had managed to barter some eggs for material, a white organdie spotted with pink, and with this she had made the prettiest dress and bonnet I had ever seen. She had even made the doll knickers to match. I was so proud. But dolls could not go to bed with us in case we rolled over onto them and broke them. I think it was more likely the dolls would pay us back with bruises, but this was Mother's excuse, which we accepted. So, following my example, Elizabeth sat her Ted next to my doll on the box and from their vantage point they watched us drop off to sleep. What high jinks those toys enjoyed that night. So excited must they have been that they forgot where they had been seated. The next morning we were aghast. They had moved. Our faces were so serious in our belief that Mother played along with us, telling us stories of how toys come into their own at night while we are asleep. For nights afterwards we would not have them in the bedroom. It was ages before we realised she had moved them in order to get something out of the box and had forgotten to replace them exactly as we had left them. How innocent children are!

That box was just like a pirate's treasure chest. It was larger of course but it had a hump-shaped lid and whenever we tried to sit on it we would invariably slide off. However, it was the contents which I was anxious to examine. It was Mother's box, out of bounds to me, but, as with all untouchables, the desire to touch is stronger. So it was, after Elizabeth was asleep, I crept out of bed and gingerly lifted the lid, and what treasure indeed did I find. I gave no heed to the warning constantly given in our household: "You'll have your nose blacked," which was a punishment for all to see if we had looked where we had no right to look or inquired where it was none of our business. Although I had frequently stood in front of the mirror watching to see my nose turn black it had not happened yet so I suppose my curiosity could not have been of sufficient depth up until now to alter the colour which nature had bestowed on me. Sweets were rationed. Only a few could be bought each month and I suppose it was Father's coupons which allowed him to buy a whole box of liqueur chocolates. I had never seen anything like it before. All those little bottles wrapped in a variety of coloured foils, red, silver, green, blue and gold, each bearing a different label: cherry brandy, crème de menthe, advocat, and so on. I could not resist the temptation to see what they were like. As silently as I could I unfolded a wrapper and there was the cutest little chocolate bottle. My ears strained to hear a movement either from Elizabeth's bed or from downstairs but all was quiet. I began to nibble the top. It was delicious. Gradually nibbling away I reached the "drink". Oh what a glorious taste and what lovely crunchy sugar lined the bottle. No-one would know if I helped myself to another one, there were so many they could never have been counted, and there I sat engrossed. A movement below made me dive for my bed and when Mother shortly called up "What are you doing?" my obvious answer, which is universal, was "Nothing". "Good nights" were repeated and I was left to dream sweet dreams. Of course, once having discovered the bounty I was nightly addicted until I realised the contents of the box had diminished to such an extent that questions were bound to be asked, but if Mother ever realised she said nothing. Perhaps she thought Father was enjoying himself when he arrived at week-ends and maybe Father thought Mother was enjoying herself when alone waiting for him to come!

In spite of all my misdemeanours, my thefts, my lies, I continued to attend morning service at the church, taking my sister along with me. If ever anyone needed forgiveness I did and I ought to have gone with the express intention of asking for it. If I had only listened more earnestly to the sermons before, perhaps I would not have strayed so easily from the straight and narrow path. Mrs. Bourne must have wondered how I had plucked up the courage to enter the church knowing what dreadful thoughts filled my mind, what unkindness I had shown in my heart. Mrs. Amies must have wondered how I dared to enter the church after all the lies I had told. Perhaps that is why Mother insisted on my going, to ask forgiveness for all my wickedness. Nevertheless, to church we went every Sunday morning dressed in our Sunday best. As a matter of fact we looked rather smart for Mother had managed to buy me a pale grey flannel suit with a double-breasted jacket and a wide-brimmed felt hat to match. She liked to see us dressed alike so she had set to and made Elizabeth a grey suit since she had been unable to buy one her size. Suits were not made for five year olds and that is why we were rather outstanding in our appearance. It would have been better under the circumstances had we – me in particular – not been so obvious, but that was the way it was and two girls dressed in grey with felt hats on their heads walked demurely along Jewkes Lane every Sunday morning on their way to Matins.

Mother did try very hard to bring us up in the Christian way of life. I think she succeeded – eventually.

It was alright going to church but coming home was a different kettle of fish. I could not bring myself to speak civilly to my sister for she had made a laughing stock of me, in church too. I had enough to contend with without suffering humiliation on her account. Yet Elizabeth had behaved herself immaculately. It was just that she had such a loud voice. I know she could not read, I know she did not know the hymns, but every time we stood to sing a hymn did she have to stand on the seat of the pew in order to see and be seen and, at the top of her voice, sing "God Save the King?" She attracted the attention of every member of the congregation and no matter how I tried to make her sit down and be quiet it had no effect. She tried to join in all the harder. It was Father's fault. Whenever the national anthem was played over the radio we had to be patriotic and follow his example in standing up to attention and singing it along with him. It was played so frequently as a morale booster it is no wonder my sister had learnt it off by heart and, having done so, she was proud to sing it as loud as she could in church, standing to attention just as everyone else did. It was preposterous.

CHAPTER X

"Monday, Tuesday, Monday, Tuesday,…" Anyone hearing us calling so outside the cottage could be excused for thinking we were playing a game, for such games were in vogue. With a skipping rope we would jump in singing "Salt, pepper, mustard, vinegar," or "Rich man, poor man, beggar man, thief," and it sounded like just another variation. Or perhaps it could be suggested we did not quite know what day it was and by repetition the right one would present itself to us. But no, both conclusions would be way out. We were instead calling our cats, Monday, the mother, and Tuesday, the son. As with most families, animals played their part. For many country children their animals belonged to the farm. The cat would be kept in the barn for the sole purpose of catching the mice and the dog would be either a watch dog chained to a kennel outside the house or a farm helper to lend a hand in rounding up the sheep and cattle, when he was not lying lazily in the sun in the farmyard, that is. So perhaps we could be excused for being rather different in that we owned no farm and were really townies, although we tried so hard to belong. However, Monday arrived as a stray and stayed as a pet and, as Robinson Crusoe had found out long before when he christened his companion Friday, if a name does not exist what better than to use the day of the week on which the subject was found or delivered or arrived, therefore what better name than "Monday" for the black cat which arrived just then?

We had found mouse trails in the cottage and had for some time set traps to catch the culprits. The surprise of the springing wire was successful at first and one or two of the vermin were eliminated but let no-one dare tell me that mice cannot learn, for our variety were adept at it. First of all they learnt to leave the traps alone and forego the cheese, delicious though it smelt. Then they discovered a way of removing the cheese without disturbing the spring so leaving us patiently waiting for the click to tell us the trap had sprung while they were laughing their heads off eating the cheese! Undaunted, we moved the traps around the house in the hope that the surprise of a new position would catch them unawares but they were too clever for us. The traps were withdrawn and Monday moved in. Our hopes were high. Days and weeks passed by but no mice were caught – at least we found no evidence, though admittedly their trails were fewer – but Monday was keeping the peace on all sides. We were happy to feel that we were winning the battle of the vermin. The mice were content to let sleeping cats lie but were wary of her when she came out to play with them, chasing them round the property and patting them along when she reached them, a mouser indeed! Pets certainly do not work for a living. Shortly after this, to our surprise, Monday was delivered of a tom kitten, a tabby one, beautifully mottled black, brown, white and ginger. The happening took place on a Tuesday so, following the same tradition, he was bestowed with the name Tuesday.

When a meal is set out the diners are inevitably called so "Monday, Tuesday", Monday, Tuesday," came the summons from the cottage. Mother was looking for them everywhere. She even went into the outhouse at the back (the building through which everyone passed to "spend a penny") when horror struck her. We had been out for the afternoon. Now Peter, the dog, a mongrel puppy in the in-between stage of canine adolescence, more than a pup and less than a dog, had, as usual when we went out, been chained to his kennel at the rear. This was a necessity as he could not be left in the cottage while we were out and to let him roam free was to ask for trouble. In a flash he would have been over the fence and in no time at all would have been a target for the farmers' guns, a sheep worrier. The sight before Mother was utter destruction. Peter was no longer chained to his kennel. He had bitten through the links, and strewn around the outhouse and all over the garden were items of clothing. Maybe Monday and Tuesday had annoyed Peter since they were allowed to roam freely and, in desperation, he had gnawed through his chain. Having achieved this perhaps he had chased them till they fled, upsetting the baskets of clothes awaiting the next washday and all the other articles previously stacked so tidily. In any event, the cats were not to be found. The dog was sitting beside his abode looking rather sheepish and worn out and the ground was littered with garments.

We came to Mother's call for help. Goodness! What had happened? My father's very best maroon pullover, of which he was extremely fond, was in threads. Peter must have put his teeth in the stitches and pulled and pulled till they tore in shreds. Mother's felt hat was in the outhouse – she had unconsciously removed it from her head at some time when she was walking through the outhouse and forgotten to pick it up again afterwards. Now it had large holes dotted all over it. A pair of shoes were no longer recognisable as such and curtains which could never again be hung stretched out like fishing nets spread out to dry. We gathered up the remaining items and dumped them back in the wash basket, rather as one would put them in a dustbin for they were good for nothing else and, in despair, followed Mother indoors. How silent we all were but I guess Mother controlled herself very well.

On the following Sunday morning Peter's days were ended. Father had borrowed a shotgun from the farmer and had led Peter away for the last time. We strained our ears to hear the one single shot but Father was very kind. He was out of our range of hearing. Some while later he returned rather soberly and in that vein the day drew gradually to its close. In bed that night my games of vision gave way to thoughts of Peter. Yes, it was a dreadful thing to have done, especially when clothing could only be obtained if one had the required number of coupons and replacements could be ill-afforded, but to shoot him was very drastic. Would he have felt any pain? No, Father was too kind for that. Was he a good shot? He had had no experience to my knowledge, not like the farmers who shot rabbits for I had watched them for hours, from a safe distance of course.

Coming home from school one afternoon last summer I had heard the "phutting" of a tractor in the distance. Gradually as I neared home, the sound grew louder till I came up alongside the field where it was at work, drawing behind it the great wooden revolving wheels used at that time in corn-cutting operations. It was harvest time on a lovely hot, late-summer afternoon and seeing people standing around in the field I jumped off my bike (for I was now the proud owner of a sparkling new two-wheeler) and leaned it against the hedge on the roadside in order to get a better vantage point to view the proceedings. I climbed the gate and stood transfixed. Every man in that field had a gun under his arm. There were women standing chatting around the perimeter so I supposed it was safe to stand here. These farmers obviously were not out looking for poachers like the Froggatt's gamekeeper so there was no chance of me being a target for them, not with so many other folks around too. As the tractor went round and round the field, gradually reducing the standing corn by a machine-width each time, the area of corn in the middle became smaller and smaller and more prominently rectangular. The standing corn was now down to about an eighth of the total and the tractor was withdrawn. The figures standing around sprang to life, men at the ready, and women doing a most peculiar war-like dance, clapping their hands and shouting. What could be the purpose of such behaviour was quite beyond me - until there was a movement beside the corn and a bang at one and the same time. Again and again at irregular intervals the gun shots were heard, sometimes so close as to sound like an echo one of another. Each time there was a shot it was followed by a click as a gun was cocked for further sport. Yet this was not sport to the farmers, it was a necessary means of ridding the countryside of vermin, for this is how rabbits were looked upon. Granted, those farmers were assured of a good supper thereafter but rabbits were destructive animals when they were allowed to breed uncontrolled. They would completely demolish a field of greens for which the farmer had hoped to receive a good price. As the corn had fallen to the harvester so the rabbits had been driven closer and closer into the centre of the field till at last there was nowhere else to go and, in an effort to escape, when the tractor was withdrawn they would run for the cover of the hedges, unaware of the fate to befall them. So, these thoughts went round and round in my mind, guns and rabbits, guns and dogs, guns and poachers, until weary of puzzling over the rights and wrongs of it all I fell asleep.

"Get down, quick, under the hedge. Don't move." I pushed Elizabeth before me. There we lay, Betty, Michael, my sister and me, hardly daring to breathe, never moving a muscle. We had dived for cover on my command, each lying full length under the low branches, regardless of the red earth and dried leaves and prickles beneath us. Frightened to move lest we attracted attention, Betty whispered "Where are they?"

"Coming down Pigeon Hill."

"Are they coming this way?"

"Yes. Shh!" I answered in a hoarse whisper.

Elizabeth began to be a little afraid. "I want to go home."

"Not now, not yet, you can't. Keep still and you'll be alright. They won't notice you then."

"They" came towards the road. "They're looking this way," said Michael and all four faces were buried in the earth hoping and praying we hadn't been spotted.

Betty breathed "They are going the other way."

Cautiously I raised my head and let out my breath and slowly each one of us crept out from our refuge.

"Do you really think they'd have shot us?" asked Elizabeth.

"Of course, if they'd seen us." Why, had I not watched the farmers shooting to kill only a quarter of a mile away up the road? When farmers were out shooting rabbits they fired at the slightest movement. They could not wait for the animal to prove what it was, otherwise it would be gone. I know, I had tried to catch them myself. So it was only sensible to dive for cover and lie perfectly still so as not to be mistaken for a rabbit! I wonder what those farmers must have thought seeing us all lying flat out on the ground, for see us they must have done. Little would they have guessed it was on their account. Rabbits indeed! As if we could ever have been mistaken for rabbits! What idiotic notions I had.

It must have been drummed into us at school and at home that guns were weapons of destruction, after all it was wartime and I took

94

everything so seriously. "If ever enemy planes fly over lie down flat on the ground. This way you will attract less attention." That was it. That was where I had learnt about attracting less attention. This rule was one of our safety code rules, just as road safety rules are learnt now, and I always tried to put into practice exactly what I had been taught. That is why I ended up under the hedge on another occasion. I was walking home up the road instead of the meadow when the drone of a plane reached my ears. At first I was not bothered but, as it grew louder and came close, I realised it was flying very low, probably on the look-out for target areas. What on earth was I to do? Why I imagined I was a sure target I have no idea but I believed it was me the plane was looking for. (It was always the plane that was the enemy, never the occupants.) I was out of reach of home. I could never get there before the plane spotted me. My heart beat faster and faster as I searched my mind for the appropriate rule. Then I knew it. I flung myself down under the hedge, face buried in the grass, waiting for the worst to happen. I listened as the plane drew closer. I waited as it passed overhead. Nothing happened. I raised my head to watch it disappear over the orchard trees and not until all sound had gone did I make for home at top speed to tell of the appearance of the enemy aeroplane I had just witnessed. "Did you, dear?" said Mother when my words had finished tumbling out over one another. "Perhaps you were mistaken; perhaps it was one of ours." I do not think that probability had ever occurred to me.

CHAPTER XI

Lords and ladies held their court under the hedge on the road leading up to ABC, at least, the lords-and-ladies that I knew did, for they were those beautiful wild flowers at other times known as cuckoo-pint.

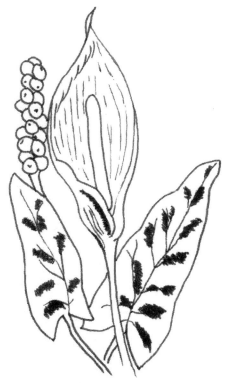

Lords and Ladies

Walking up the road I was searching for the pale yellow-green petal standing tall and pointed and curving protectively around its central tongue of red, guarding it, shielding it from harm. There were only a few growing beneath the hedge and while the rain dripped from the trees above, occasionally the drops finding their way inside my collar to my discomfort, I walked along poking this way and that in order to find them and make sure they were still there. The smell of the wet earth was everywhere and accompanied me through the orchard until I reached home where it was replaced by the smell of damp clothes around the fire. Mother was ironing those garments which had dried and placing them on the clothes' horse before the fire where the steam rose, giving off such a sweet clean smell. This was a pleasant homecoming after a damp journey home. Here was such a warmth and cosiness in the cottage.

On other days, later in the year, my homeward journey would be interrupted by my search for the wild orchids which grew in abundance at the bottom of the meadow. I was on the last lap of the day's trek, out of the clutches of the boys who had gradually dwindled in number as they arrived at their homes en route, and was glad to be able to dawdle and pursue my own activities unimpeded. Those delightful little purple orchids were the next best species to the king-cups and, added to the gigantic ox-eyed daisies, those smiling white faces surrounding a cushion of gold, made bouquets fit for a queen and, thus armed with nosegays of wild flowers, I would arrive home to greet my mother.

The greeting was not exchanged, though, on this day. I had reached home to find the house empty. As usual, I went through the door singing, for again, as usual, the door stood wide open in welcome. "Hello," I called, but there was no reply. I glanced in the living room and kitchen but they were unoccupied. "She must be round the back," I muttered to myself for "round the back" meant pursuing that occupation in which she delighted so much, the gorgeous job which was so therapeutic, the sawing up of wood. But there came no sound of activity from that direction. I wandered round to the outhouse calling for her to no avail, then returning to the front I stood still to collect my thoughts. The door was open. The key was still in the lock. There was no note of explanation. She could not have gone far, perhaps a walk to the gate or down the meadow to meet us. Elizabeth had lagged behind. Perhaps if Mother had walked down the road she would have met her by now and they would be making their way up the path. I retraced my steps to the stile but no-one was in sight. As I turned again towards the house doubts crept into my mind. As it was wartime suppose the Germans had landed and taken her away whilst I was at school. Goodness! What would we do without her? The cottage had looked tidy enough. They had not bothered with anything else except Mother. I began to get panicky but that would not help anyone. I would be brave. I would go into the house to think. Carefully stepping into the hall I listened for alien sounds. There were none. I peered expectantly into each room downstairs fearful of finding an unknown face, an enemy waiting to pounce on me. There was no-one. The latch on the gate clicked. I stood still. Feet trod the pathway to the front door. I dared not breathe and when Elizabeth merrily shouted her greeting I relaxed like a rag doll with relief. But she was alone. She had not seen Mother at all. I could not share my fear with her for she was too young and I was now in charge so, while I wondered, we waited. Then Mother appeared alone. I was so relieved and, perhaps owing to my own relief, I was unconscious of the sad expression on her face. "Where have you been? I looked all over the place for you and couldn't find you. I thought you couldn't have gone far as you didn't lock the door." I did not mention the Germans.

"I'm sorry I wasn't here when you got home. I didn't have time to leave a note, but I'm back now so all's well."

"Where did you go? We didn't see you."

"No, you couldn't because I went with Grandma to the hospital."

"Oooh." That word escaped as a long-drawn-out sound and enough had been said. Why had I not looked to see if Grandma was alright upstairs when I came home, I wondered? I suppose because I was so anxious about Mother. This was the last visit Grandma paid to our cottage. My maternal grandparents, Grandma and Grandpa Adams, lived in Birmingham and had experienced the bombing raids around their home. A fortnight previously Grandpa had phoned through to the farm. The message which reached us was: Could Grandma come down for a holiday, she was not very well? So it was arranged that Father should collect her in the car and bring her to stay the very next week-end. She could stay till she was better. I was pleased, remembering the cosy evenings in the armchair of her last holiday spent with us. We all waited expectantly on the Saturday evening for the car to arrive but what a shock Mother had. When her mother had left us not long ago she was cheerfully waving "Goodbye". Now she was thin and so pale. Why, what could have happened? The doctor who was summoned wondered at her arriving alive and, as he glared at my father, he accused "It's a wonder you didn't bring a corpse with you!" She ought never to have faced the journey in her state. Hot water bottles were put in the bed immediately and, with all the help we could give, she retired to bed. She was suffering from shock, shock from the bombs which had dropped all around her home. This shock, along with diabetes from which she unknowingly suffered, had reduced her to this pathetic figure. For a fortnight Mother had tended to her needs, acceded to her demands. These became more and more frequent as she was for ever thirsty. As soon as she had been helped to a drink and the cup replaced on the saucer she cried out for more. She was desperate for water but we could never satisfy her craving. Mother would sit beside her for hours, moistening her lips in an attempt to ease her distress. Gradually, day by day, she weakened till at last she fell into a coma and the doctor arranged for her to be moved to the Tenbury Cottage Hospital three and a half miles away. The ambulance had called and Mother had accompanied Grandma on her last journey from the cottage. That was where she had been.

For three weeks Grandma lay in a coma in the hospital and each day Mother would cycle down the three and a half miles to visit her. Most times it would be during the day while we were at school but occasionally she would go in the early evening, leaving me in charge. One afternoon during her third week there Mother decided to go earlier in the day than usual and, as she was pushing her bike through the orchard to the gate, Tom, our landlord's son, came walking towards her. He had a message. A telephone call had just come through from Tenbury. Grandma had died without regaining consciousness. Mother thanked Tom and cycled on all the way into town for her last visit to the Cottage Hospital, and we had seen Grandma for the last time.

CHAPTER XII

"Are you ready yet? Do hurry up, we'll be late," called Mother standing impatiently at the front door, key in hand, waiting to lock it. She would never lose that key for it weighed about half-a-pound. She dared not lose it. There was only one and it was practically impossible to duplicate. About six inches long and made of iron, one was well aware of it in one's pocket. When they had first received it on the day they took over the tenancy of ABC my parents had stared in disbelief at its enormous size and, after glancing at each other, had burst out laughing.

"We shall never lose that one, that's for sure," was Father's emphatic comment.

I breathlessly appeared, tugging on my gloves. "Have you got your shoes, both of you?" Mother queried anxiously.

"I have, and you've got Elizabeth's," I remarked, for Mother was inclined to forget what she had got and what she had not! Pushing my bike through the gate I then endeavoured to hold the two, bike and gate, so that Mother and Elizabeth could pass through, struggling down the two steps with my sister's bike. I had had mine for my ninth birthday earlier in the year and was very proud of it. As I was unable to manage a full-sized bike Father had chosen a slightly smaller one but it was a bike with a difference. Everyone else's had a straight frame where ladies dismounted but mine was curved. The boys and girls at school did not quite know what to make of it and eagerly watched as I got on and off to show how I could do it without getting my toe caught on the bar. I told them it was shaped specially for me! How gullible they were. I was determined to dismount taking my foot behind the line of the body and appearing to scoot the last step - I was an adept scooter as I knew! All country ladies took their foot through in front, raised themselves from the saddle and daintily walked off their bike. Not me! There was the same difference as riding side-saddle or astride a horse. I was the astride type!

It was early on a Saturday morning and we were off on our trek to town as we had been in the habit of doing every Saturday morning for the last twelve months. Sometimes Mother took the pram in order to rest Elizabeth's tiring legs. At other times my sister would go on her own bicycle, a fairy cycle, for, of course, I had made her learn to ride my bike by standing her on the pedals and pushing her till she could balance. It was considered an advantage for her to have her own bike to help us on our travels. On these days Mother would swing along beside the two of us until her younger daughter's legs grew tired of spinning round and round at twice the speed of sound, for on a small bike one inevitably pedals much faster in order to keep up. Then Elizabeth would just sit stationary and Mother was obliged to bend down and push behind the low saddle till she felt her back would break, knowing that on reaching our destination she would have great difficulty in unwinding. The return journey was not even to be thought of. Along the road we would go, wending our way past cow pancakes and clods of mud. No-one would pass us, no-one greet us, for Aston Bank Cottage was the cottage at the end of the road. We went down the meadow to school and joined Jewkes Lane at the bottom, but the route to Tenbury lay in front of our house, the road to Aston Bank. As we passed the various farms we looked in vain for signs of life. We always hoped to discover the place where the Big Car was parked and had a vague idea we would see it at

Aston Court. Occasionally, as we returned home from church on a Sunday morning, two girls dressed in grey and only on those days when accompanied by Mother carrying the can of milk (for milk had to be fetched whatever the day, whatever the weather) the Big Limousine would draw up beside us and the gentlewoman would graciously ask if they could give us a lift. They knew who we were and where we came from but, to this day, their identity has eluded us. "But we have the milk with us and it might spill" was insufficient reason for declining the offer so generously given, and so, brushing the last spec of dust from our shoes, we climbed into the rear of the car and travelled the distance home in state, Mother perched upright in the centre of the back seat holding the can of milk before her, trembling lest the movement would sway the can, slopping the contents over the side. She quaked lest she spilt one drop to mar the interior of this beautiful vehicle.

Some Saturdays I would have to take this road alone, should my sister be unfit to make the journey, for, although she was in marvellous health compared to her previous state, she still did not have much stamina. I enjoyed cycling along, that is until I reached the point where the army had encamped. The army personnel kept to themselves and we had nothing to do with them. Someone in that camp owned a brute of a dog built on the lines of a boxer. That dog had one sport and for this he would wait a whole week. He would lie in wait for me to arrive and, as I approached, he would gradually stalk to the gateway. At this point I had weighed up the situation and would vary my procedure from week to week. It was either a cut and thrust job when I would cycle furiously and gather as much speed as possible in order to shoot past the camp and be gone before the animal realised I was coming, or travel slowly in order to dismount and walk past him, fooling him into thinking he could not scare me. Both strategies failed. If I sped past he would rush out to attack me, frantically barking, attracted by the sparkling, madly revolving wheels, and the only way in which I could prevent him from having his nose minced was to kick out at him to frighten him away, thus laying myself open for a return attack. If I walked past he was there waiting and he would approach my bike, nose stretched forward, tracing the rim of the wheel in anticipation of his expected enjoyment. I do not know which variation frightened me most, but, as soon as that dog admitted defeat and gave up the chase, slowly turning his attention once again in the direction of the camp, I would begin to pedal fast and furiously till I was round the corner out of sight, thankful that I lived to face another day.

By this time we had reached the notorious Aston Bank. "Get off your bikes and walk down. Keep in to the side, both of you." It was a straight drop down under the railway bridge to the main Tenbury Road at the bottom. Mother was always fearful of us being unable to control our bikes and certainly on those days when I did try out my brakes my hands ached with the effort and I was very willing to walk the last part of the downward gradient. We had to keep in in case a car came and, if a car came, in case the driver lost control. It was as bad as that! Some years after, we were to learn that Connie, who was of the nearest neighbour's family, met an untimely death as she cycled down the hill. As Mother had feared on our account, Connie's brake cables snapped and immediately she careered downwards gathering momentum till she ran into the path of a car on the main road at the bottom.

Once on the Tenbury road the going was flat, though long and winding, but our goal was visible over the fields in the distance. Passing between the Peacock Inn and the River Teme, where Grandpa Adams often used to fish in his younger days, we would step over the line in the road where Worcestershire County Council stopped their steam roller rolling the chippings into the tar and Shropshire County Council began, neither trespassing on the other's property. At last we would reach the bridge over the river and enter the country town of Tenbury, as one would traverse the drawbridge of a castle, past the shops, each of which meant something special to me, right through the town, to a dim little courtyard at the rear of one of the houses and here, in a bare dusty room, was the reason for our ninety-minute trek. The dancing class was in progress.

Dancing began for me at the age of four in the lounge of an acquaintance of Mother's.

At Mrs. Davis' in Birmingham, "Ten Pretty Girls",
Peggy Davis on the left, Sheila Henderson second left,
Brenda Pugh on the right and me kneeling in front.

We had even given a show for parents and friends in a hired hall and I had actually played the part of a fairy in a dance called "Ten Pretty Girls." I was no lightweight and therefore not very fairy-like but, with time and devotion as fairy godmothers will tell, my appearance was changed. I no longer deserved the title "Miss Tailor-Made" and my plaits had been screwed round rags during the preceding nights till I emerged with curls and ringlets around my shoulders. Another dance had seen me as soloist, dancing round a small Scottie dog and, although this centrepiece was a toy, I was able to believe in its reality since my own Scottie had acted as understudy during my practice hours at home! Therefore I entered this country school as a veteran, showing Elizabeth how to dance this way and that. We rehearsed at the cottage over and over again for I was a perfectionist and my pupil must go over and over her performance until she could not be faulted unless she dropped from exhaustion beforehand. The consequence was disastrous. We were to give a concert at The Bridge Hotel on this side of the river in Tenbury, all the pupils taking part, and to this end we rehearsed unfailingly. On the appointed night the curtain rose and the audience clapped their appreciation as each item was concluded. Then came our embarrassment: "The sun has got his hat on, hip, hip, hip, hooray," we all sang, touching our hats at the appropriate moment and opening our mouths like fish so that all the words could be heard. The audience applauded. Then Elizabeth, quite lost as to where she was and the significance of the occasion and so used to repeating her performance over and over again, did just that. As we all danced off the stage she took it into her head to do a repeat performance, oblivious of the stage whispers calling her off and all hands beckoning her to come. On she continued, tapping her hat, singing at the top of her voice - thank goodness she had not called the show to a close with her rendering of "God Save the King" – till, as a last resort, the teacher had to walk on stage herself and drag her off crying. I do believe she had the loudest applause of all but she was my sister and I was mortified.

The most eagerly awaited moment of those Saturdays came after our lesson. At the end of the street of shops was the cleanest, most appealing little house I knew. Yet it was not as a house that I knew it for the front room had been turned into a café and it always seemed to beckon to me as I approached it, wanting to invite me in. The window twinkled in the sunlight and the half net curtain, peculiar to cafés, dazzled one's eyes with its whiteness. The café simply exuded cleanliness. No-one ever seemed to go in or come out, not while I was looking longingly in that direction, but I would catch sight of the proprietor who was both waitress and owner of the house, peeping over the top of the curtain seeking prospective customers. After repeated requests for refreshment, which were always turned down either on account of the cost or the time, the day arrived when we were allowed to approach the glossy black door with its polished brass knocker. With an expectant air we tripped up the two steps and were smilingly directed to the seat in the window. The owner in her black dress and white frilly apron beamed as she lowered her head to hear our order and efficiently jotted it down on her note pad. "Beans on toast for three please." This was living in the lap of luxury. Heinz baked beans were new to us. We had never tasted anything like them before and could hardly sit still while waiting for our order to be despatched. Our waitress disappeared behind the scenes to grill the toast and cook the beans and re-appeared quite unflustered, face still beaming smiles all round, with a tray on which were three plates steaming with hot baked beans. No word was spoken as we savoured our lunch. A treat to end all treats, as this was, must be enjoyed to the full. In due course we left the café lovingly looking all around us, to think we had been inside at last. What a wonderful day it was.

We passed the grocer's shop where Mrs. Dyke served. She was the lady who came to collect our grocery order. Every Thursday, whatever the weather, Mrs. Dyke would set off from the shop on her bicycle, order book and pencils in the basket. We all had baskets strapped to our handlebars; they were so useful for popping things in. Saddlebags were all very well but only so much could be put in there before the straps had to be fastened. On the other hand, baskets on the front could be piled up dangerously high and by guiding the bike with one hand the other was free to catch any item which looked ready to disengage itself. Mrs. Dyke toured the surrounding countryside calling at each house where she knew a customer would be waiting for her. After a chat and a cup of tea the order would be given. First the rations were listed – bacon, butter, margarine, lard, cheese, tea and sugar. Only so much of each commodity was allowed per person each week and, so that no-one exceeded his allowance, an appropriate coupon would be removed from the ration book.

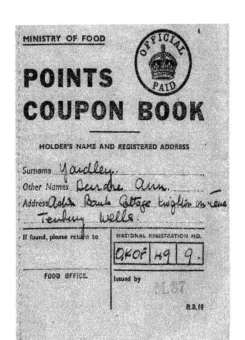

MINISTRY OF FOOD

OFFICIAL PAID

POINTS
COUPON BOOK

HOLDER'S NAME AND REGISTERED ADDRESS

Surname *Yardley.*
Other Names *Deirdre Ann.*
Address *Cobb. Bank Cottage knighton on teme*
Tenbury Wells.

If found, please return to

FOOD OFFICE.

NATIONAL REGISTRATION NO.

QKOF 49 9.

Issued by

R.B.19

NOTES.

1.—You can use these coupons at any retailers you choose. You must always have the book with you when you use them and the retailer will cut them out. You must not cut them out yourself.

2.—You will be told from time to time for what foods they are needed and what are the values in points of coupons marked "A," "B," "C."

3.—There are four coupons marked "A" on both sides, four marked "B" and four marked "C."

4.—The periods for which the coupons are available are already marked. They cannot be used outside these four-week periods.

5.—You can deposit any of the rows of coupons if you and the retailer wish. If you do this you should note on page 15 where you deposited them and you must fill in your name where indicated on the coupon pages.

If you deposit these coupons with a retailer you must fill in overleaf.

If you deposit these coupons with a retailer you must fill in overleaf.

If you deposit these coupons with a retailer you must fill in overleaf.

If you deposit these coupons with a retailer you must fill in overleaf.

ANYTHING ON THIS YOU DEPOSIT ROWS WITH A RETAILER.

with Retailer. and Address).	Initials of Retailer.

My Food Coupon Book

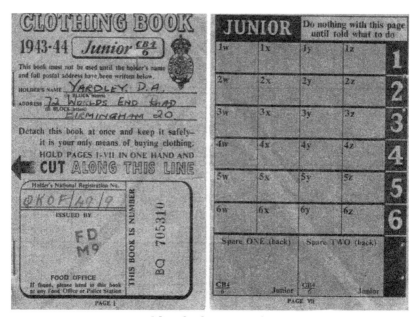

My Clothing Book

At the beginning of the war everyone was issued with an identity number which appeared on the front of all their ration books. Mine, committed to memory, was QKOF 49/9

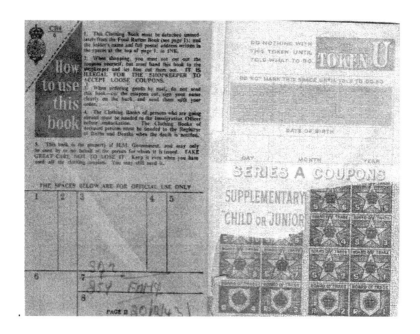

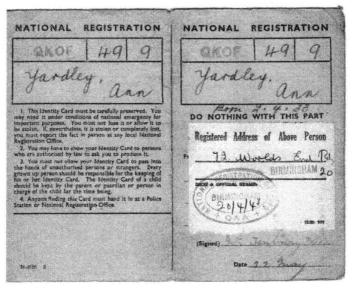

My Identity Card.

There were ration books for food and clothing. Everyone bought everything which was allocated, regardless of likes and dislikes, with a view to trading the undesirables with someone willing to exchange for something else. After the rations any extras would be added according to the number of coupons one had left in the ration book for that month. When the order was completed Mrs. Dyke would set off for the next farm or cottage on her route and, at the end of her day, would return to the shop to have the orders made up ready for the little van to deliver them on Saturday. Thursday, though, was always referred to as "Mrs. Dyke's Day."

We looked in the windows of the Gentlemen's Outfitters for it was from here that Mother had been able to obtain our grey felt hats. She had enquired at numerous other more likely shops, or so she thought, for headwear for us, only to meet with a negative answer, for country children did not go in for anything like that, only the gentry, and they did not shop here. As she was passing this Gentlemen's Outfitters wondering where to try next she saw the hats adorning a corner of the window. "That's just what I'm looking for," she exclaimed, and inside we all went. They were perfect. They were the sort preparatory school boys may have worn before caps became the universal head covering! People certainly looked twice in our direction as we passed.

The little wool shop up the two steps was always a magnet to my mother and she would come out with a bag containing grey sock wool for another pair of three-quarter socks for each of us. Those hand knitted socks were so warm and comfortable and since the General's lady thought nothing of walking round the country lanes busily clicking her needles, a ball of wool tucked under her arm, Mother accepted it as the done thing and followed suit, for not only had she our socks to do but Father's as well. Is it any wonder then that I also followed in my mother's footsteps, especially after my success with the War Effort?

This was the farmers' wives' market day and an open market was held at the back of the town but the atmosphere on Saturday was very different to Tuesday, the latter being the farmers' market day. The segregation was unintentional, merely a matter of quantity over quality, for on Tuesday the livestock market, up by the doctors, was brought into its own and town was full of the bleating of sheep, the mooing of cows and squeals from the pigs, all being herded into the pens. I suggest this market was so situated as to be convenient for farmers, shocked by the exchange of animals for money and vice versa, to be treated by the doctor before returning home to divulge the day's dealings! Others would say it was situated opposite the hotel bar where they could wallow in misery or share their profits amongst their fellow farmers. Each may draw his own conclusions. Today we were on our bikes and had to cycle back home while Mother walked alongside but the procedure on Tuesday was altogether different. A single-decker green bus would be seen travelling through the country lanes, stopping every now and then to pick up its passengers. Mother would make her way to Mrs. Amies' where it was arranged she would embark at around two o'clock. I was generally at school but in her before-school days Elizabeth either accompanied Mother to town or stayed behind with Auntie Nell. Now this dear old soul was a distant relative of Mrs. Amies and the two of them had lived together ever since we had known them and long before that. Auntie Nell never went out but was happy to potter around the garden in the sunshine when she was not helping Mrs. Amies in the house. The latter had little that was good to say about Auntie Nell and indicated she was over the hill, a little senile in her behaviour, which may be put down to her deafness as she could never hear a word which was spoken to her, and that she was an encumbrance. Maybe she was towards the end of her life when I remember her having to sit with her bandaged leg on a stool, unable to move out of the window which overlooked the junction but, nevertheless, if she suffered pain we did not see it on her face or hear it in her voice for she was always glad to see us and to chat and one felt her sweet smile was not a fixture but a genuine result of her happiness at being alive. She liked to look after my sister just as Elizabeth loved to keep Auntie Nell company. They understood each other. They were kindred spirits you might say.

If Mrs. Amies was not at the door waiting for the bus on these Tuesday afternoons, then the driver would get out to find out why. He had no intention of travelling to town minus any of his regulars unless there was a valid reason. There was the old man who lived past the inn who was not outside when the bus approached. Out jumped the driver and knocked on his door to see if he was alright. When the old man explained that he was not coming today the driver asked what he should bring back for him. The employees of this company certainly rendered a service. One-man buses are all the rage these days but there was only ever one employee of the bus company on our bus. A conductor was unheard of out here. As you stepped onto the bus you paid the driver, no argument about the correct fare or you got off, and while he was sorting out the change he would ask how the family was and if little Johnny was better today. How pleasant were those days when life was not one great rush? At one cottage the farmer's wife locked her door, ran down the path and boarded the bus only to discover she had left her gloves behind in the house. The bus was stopped while she ran back, unlocked the door, picked up her gloves and came out, locking up once again behind her and breathlessly came aboard. There were smiles of satisfaction all round.

Once in Tenbury, everyone went about their business, gradually filling up their baskets as they progressed from one shop to another. Then the strangest thing happened. When a basket became too heavy to carry it was placed on the pavement at the bus stop and was left there unattended until the bus came along while its owner continued to shop. The thought would never enter her head that all the contents might not be just as she had left them. Why should it? No basket was ever disturbed. A strange sight it would seem today to have a queue of overloaded shopping baskets lined up at the kerbside with no owner in view to guard them. On those occasions when Elizabeth went to town too, after the shopping had been completed and the basket parked, my mother would take her down to the riverside and there they would spend the time throwing stones in the waster, skimming them and playing ducks and drakes until the scheduled time of the departure drew near. With a bus loaded with passengers and twice as heavy with their goods, the driver would set off once more and this time, instead of knocking doors to see where his passengers had got to, he would help them off the bus and carry their loads to their door, throwing a parting shot at them: "Be sure to be ready on time next week."

CHAPTER XIII

The long summer holidays were wonderful, stretching before us full of surprises awaiting our investigation. Jewkes Lane shimmered in the heat and Pigeon Hill began to look like heathland where the dry grasses provided cover for the habitat of many varied insects. We were used to the sound of grasshoppers, their chirping made as they rubbed their hind legs against their wings, but the sound we now heard as we crept along the road puzzled us. It was a grating sound, similar, but certainly not the same, as the grasshoppers. We followed the noise searching among the dry tufts of grass but were unable to trace the cause until we returned by this route later in the week. Then we saw the corpse. Someone had been more successful than we had. They had found their quarry and killed it, probably believing it to be a poisonous reptile. Its stiff green body, about nine inches long, lay at the side of the road, its warning sound now silent, for what we had tried to find unsuccessfully was there before us, a harmless grass snake.

When we were not creeping along after insects we were riding our bikes or I was letting my friends take turns on my scooter.

Elizabeth on her bike in the orchard

My scooter was a beautiful toy, if it could be classified as such, for I often used it as transport to and from school or Tenbury. It was tall and sturdy with a wide platform on which I could place both feet at the same time. Something else which mine had and others did not was a strong foot brake on the back wheel and when I stepped on it with my heel the scooter would skid to a halt. It skidded best on the loose chippings at the side of the road where they were superfluous to the road mender's needs and had not been steam-rolled into the hot, sticky tar, and the patch of road which provided the most spectacular skid was Maes Court corner. The road ran downhill from before Mrs. Amies' and continued its downward slope round the corner right to the Jewkes Lane pool, which meant I could scoot without effort for about a quarter of a mile unless I "braked" beforehand. As usual, I was demonstrating my prowess when Mother's proverbial statement bore fruit – "Pride always goes before a fall." I skidded so beautifully I could not keep my balance and the momentum of my ride prior to the skid took me travelling on while the scooter had carried out my bidding. I collected more chippings in my leg than there were freckles on my face and staggered home bewildered and bleeding, a sorry sight before all my friends. I learnt my lesson the hard way. Morning and evening from then on would see me standing on my good leg in a stork-like fashion, holding the ankle of my injured leg so that I could dip my knee into a bowl of near-boiling, disinfected water. The amount of mineral and dirt embedded in my flesh had turned my knee septic and for weeks I had to perform this contortionist act in an endeavour to get rid of the poison. There were no antibiotics to help, just disinfectant and patience. My accident endowed me with a scar which is an ever present reminder of that proverb which Mother delighted in preaching to me in order to drive home the stupidity of my performance. She still remarks that that scooter was nearly the death of her, although I was the one who suffered!

I could not ride my bike with my knee padded and bandaged so bulkily and the scooter was an unmentionable piece of equipment so my interest now became centred on the pram. Elizabeth had dispensed with it and it was stored in the outhouse but we felt it would be fun to have it out. I had pushed her in it to school so often that I fell to wondering what it would be like sitting in a pram. I could not recall the experience from my own baby days but here was an opportunity to recapture the sensation so I crawled into the pram. It was a tight squeeze but I managed just to get my head inside the hood. "Now push," I ordered Elizabeth. She huffed and puffed and pushed as hard as she could. "Come on, push harder, I am not moving."

"You're so heavy I can't make it go," she whined.

"Try again," and I bounced as much as I was able to get is started. Elizabeth did her best but she just was not strong enough and before we could think of another way to get going Mother's angry voice reached us.

"Get out of there at once, you'll ruin it. What do you think you're playing at, a great big girl like you! You'll break the pram. Where's your sense?" Oh, why did I always have to have sense? It was clear to her that the devil was finding work for idle hands so she jumped in before he could do much damage. "Get a cloth and some warm soapy water and clean the pram inside and out. Then when you've done that you can start on your bike. It could do with having some of the mud removed." So saying, she walked away leaving no doubt in my mind as to what was expected of me. Armed with cloth and warm soapy water I did as I was bid. The pram was relatively easy but my bike taxed my energy, especially in between the spokes on the rims of the wheels. I tried desperately hard to make them sparkle but, being dissatisfied with my efforts, I went to find her to seek advice. "What you need is a bit of elbow-grease," she answered. So, not to be outdone, I promptly went into the scullery and searched through the cupboards which held all the polishes. There was shoe polish, beeswax furniture polish which Mother made herself, silver polish and brass polish. There was polish for black leading and polish for the floor but on no tin could I find the appropriate wording for which I was looking - elbow grease. I decided we were out of stock and I would just make the best job of my bike that I could. When Father came home at the week-end I asked him if he had

had the elbow grease, thinking perhaps he had used it on the car. He agreed that he had but had not got any left now and a slow smile spread over his face while I explained how I had searched along the shelves for it. He told me I would have to ask for some the next time I went to the grocers. Fortunately for me the need for it had passed and I was spared the embarrassment of being laughed at. I did not realise until several years later that it was not a commodity to be bought!

One warm sunny afternoon found Mother experimenting in the fusty downstairs guest room. It had been cleared out and was airing and she had found it an ideal place with more space than anywhere else in the cottage in which to exercise to such an extent that the perspiration which was pouring down her face was hardly visible for her hair which covered it. The reason for this extreme activity on such a warm day was the state of the milk! The cow providing it must have been about to calve for the milk was so rich that half of it at least was thick cream, so thick that if you dragged your finger over the surface it would wrinkle. I do not know whether Mother disliked it being as creamy as this or whether she was exercising the economy part of her mind, but she decided to remove the cream to make some butter. It would help eke out the rations. We had no utensils for such a pastime and therefore resorted to the most primitive method. We had a milk bottle. She poured the thick cream into the milk bottle, placed the palm of her hand over the top and shook it ad infinitum. When she tired and her arms ached till she could shake no more I continued, stopping occasionally to inspect the contents of the bottle. It began to reach a solid state, first a small lump then, as our arms stepped up the movement the lump grew till no cream was left, only a watery solution besides the lump of butter. We had made some butter! For the first time then the problem was presented to us. We became aware of the size of the neck of the bottle compared with the solid contents. How were we to extract one from the other? It would not be poured out. It would not shake out. The only alternative was to scoop it out. So this we did with a long handled knife until we had transferred one lump inside the bottle to many lumps outside the bottle. All we had to do then was to pat it into shape. It did not taste like the bought butter, it had no salty taste to it and it was rather disappointing to find that all that cream made so small a pat of butter but we had achieved our aim, or rather Mother had, wondering whether all the effort was worthwhile. She was worn out and I do not remember the practice ever being repeated, presumably because the outcome did not warrant the effort involved, but we had had the experience and satisfaction of turning cream into butter.

Of the games we played and the activities we pursued perhaps the most frequent occupation was "playing at school." Gertie Cox must have been about fourteen and she lived with her elder sister and parents in the tumble-down cottage on the other side of the road at the bottom of the meadow. The prospect of playing "teacher" to three willing pupils – at least, two willing and one made to will! – drove her to leave home early in the morning and take up residence in our garden for as long as the "school" was in progress. The other pupil besides Elizabeth and me was my friend Betty Albeard who, like Gertie, preferred our garden to hers. Why, I do not know, for there was nothing pretty or attractive in it. At Mrs. Amies' Betty could enjoy the beauty of laid-out grassy paths between the trellises of roses. I believe the idea was brought over from Maes Court where the General's gardeners laboured unceasingly to produce grounds worthy of being photographed for inclusion in the country's top magazines. Here at the cottage the two patches of soil, one on either side of the front path, were coaxed to produce cabbages and cauliflowers. Instead of the perfume from flowers we were compelled to suffer the smell of the greens. However, we set up the "classroom" against the front hedge which stretched upwards till it met the branches of the damson tree and, in a secluded little area such as this, we attacked our work vigorously and with enthusiasm – far more than we had done during term time. We were models of perfection, behaviour-wise and workwise. Everything was ticked right regardless and stars were stuck on our work willy nilly. Little did our teacher realise the torment Elizabeth had gone through beforehand. She did not want to play school because she could not do the hard work we did. This was only to be expected really since she was four years younger. But a school cannot be run properly with only two in attendance, especially when a third wants to disrupt things so frequently. Therefore, Elizabeth must be helped to like it. In the hallway of the cottage, just through the front door, was a huge cupboard, the top being about level with my shoulders and, through a superhuman effort, I was able to seat my sister up on top. There she would stay until she had learnt her lessons for the day. No matter how she moaned she could not get down until she was word perfect and it behoved her to learn fast and accurately because, you see, there was no way for her to climb down. Her feet only dangled a foot from the top and she was scared stiff. She could only come down to earth with my help. What a beastly sister I was!

Gertie teaching Betty, Elizabeth and me

Gertie hearing Elizabeth read with Betty and me

Now Gertie stood at the blackboard very efficiently, chalk in one hand, pointer in the other, while we recited our tables and showed our improvement in spelling. She had Elizabeth out at the front to hear her reading while we sat bolt upright in our deck chairs, hands behind our backs, so attentively. None of these proceedings could take place, however, until one special ceremony had been performed each morning. Chairs were ready, blackboard in position, papers and pencils set out on the trestle-type bench which served as our desks and then I would disappear into the orchard and meadow scouring the hedgerows to return some minutes later with the morning's offering to teacher. I suspect she had more bouquets presented to her during those summer days than during the whole of the rest of her life.

Mother would view our activities with pleasure. She could keep her eye on us and know that we were not in any mischief but spending our time profitably. She, herself was continually being frustrated by the antics of the boiler, for attempts to get it started varied from an immediate flare up to hours of trial and error ending in nothing. Washing had to be done in the outhouse with every drop of water being pumped up from the well, carried round to the back in buckets and tipped into the boiler standing in the corner. (The boiler was like the copper in Grandma Yardley's house. Grandma Yardley was my father's mother and also lived in Birmingham. She had a huge copper basin with space beneath for the fire to heat the water.) At the cottage the paper and twigs beneath the boiler would soon catch fire and with a joyful crackling would indicate to the operative that it was ready to devour more fuel. Mother would then be madly rushing backwards and forwards to the wood pile fetching the largest, driest pieces of timber which the vicious creature could take in its ever-open mouth and, before very long, the water would be hot enough to take its load.

The winter posed a different problem. During the snow a way would first have to be shovelled round the cottage where a drift against the outhouse door would appear like a wall before one's eyes. Tunnelling through the drift would only result in the top half falling down on one's head, intent on burying the would-be washerwoman, or visitor to the toilet for that matter! Once inside fingers were blown and feet stamped in an effort to get circulation, already on the move, down to the farthest extremities. One was almost defeated before one began. Off again with the shovel to dig a path to the wood pile where one attempted to find dry tinder, the only possible place being in the heart of the stack. Undaunted, Mother groped for it and managed to reach sufficient for her immediate needs. Then began the prospect of hours of patient endeavour. The damp twigs would wet the paper but, after several sheets and half a box of matches, they would dry out sufficiently to be able to hope they would begin to burn. The fire would struggle, emitting clouds of grey smoke which blew into Mother's eyes in defiance of her acting like a pair of bellows, then with a spit of disdain it would die. Yet again she would start with more paper, for the washing could not wait till the summer and, through trial and error, struggles and strife, she would make it obey her commands. It would often be dinner time before the dratted thing was burning powerfully enough to accept damp logs and begin to heat the water. How she longed for her gas wash boiler which had had to be left back at home. But even having it here would serve no purpose since, along with the lack of electricity, we also had no gas. People living in the back of beyond could not expect to have pipes laid for their convenience. Mod. Cons. were just not on the books.

Mother was becoming eccentric. At least our near neighbours, that family which lived at the back of the orchard and intrigued me so often, may have been excused for thinking so. They heard her talking and, as no-one beside herself was there, she could only have been talking to herself. That is said to be the first sign of insanity. But they would have had greater cause for suspicion if they had known she was talking to her fire, for Mother, in her efforts to cajole it into life would often resort to talking to it. We are advised to talk to flowers to make them grow so why not try the same approach with other things? Mother was a great reader and picked up all sorts of tips from all sorts of places. I doubt whether this neighbour family were nearly so well versed. She, my Mother that is, was also known to stand outside in the moonlight in a trance – such a queer carry-on. Did they not realise she was listening to the owls hooting to one another from all sides of the orchard and was even watching the one perched up on the roof? And did not anyone else hear the nightjars calling? Country folk do not notice the beautiful happenings going on around them every day of their lives. They just take them all for granted. For instance, the dreadful muttering that issued forth when spring brought the cuckoo to our shores. They would moan because it woke them too early in the morning and drove them insane "cucking" all day long. "Cuckoo" was not a word to be spoken, it was always "That dratted bird". But my mother was otherwise affected. She waited for its first call each year and, as it became more forceful with its cries, so would she respond more joyfully. These weeks the red quarry-tiles in the hall would shine and sparkle with all the time she devoted to them for, with the door wide open, scrubbing brush in hand, bowl of soapy water and tin of polish beside her, she would scrub and polish away, calling "cuckoo" at the top of her voice in answer to the insistent call of "that dratted bird". And the more she answered it, the more frequently would it encourage her! It even came to seek its mate on the morning I was sitting outside the door enjoying the sunshine. I watched it perch on the garden fence eyeing the kneeling figure with surprise and, when it realised it had been fooled, flew off into the trees with the most indignant "cucking" I have ever heard. Our neighbours were obliged to pass the cottage whenever they left their house for there was no other way to reach the road and the children, in taking the meadow route to school, walked around two sides of our boundary outside the fence glaring through to see if anyone was around. Perhaps a sight of Mother was what they hoped for.

Sheila was the nearest in age to myself and occasionally I would stand chatting with her. There were several girls with the name of Sheila but this Sheila had a most unusual second name: she was actually Sheila Letitia. I had never heard this name before and, at first, thought it so strange. It was certainly uncommon. "Sheila Letitia", the more I said it, the more I liked the sound and long after she had disappeared from view I would be standing lost in thought, staring after her, savouring "Sheila Letitia" as I rolled it round my tongue. The family was so different to any I knew for I could not fathom out why there were so many of them. My friends were often only children or they had just one brother or sister. Occasionally I came across a family where there were three offspring and I always felt they were different to us. Keeping one sister in order was surely hard enough, how would anyone be able to cope with more? But this family boasted seven children. It was incredible. Connie was a little older than Sheila. She was very quiet and rather shy and I liked her but, owing to the age difference, we did not speak very often. The two older girls had left school and were at work and, since the family was large and the house small, spent much of their leisure time at their grandmother's. Then there was Jimmy who was younger than Sheila but, as he enjoyed the sport which the girls provided on the way home, I avoided him like the plague. The youngest was Raymond who, at three years old, would stand outside our garden fence for hours staring through the palings and what went through his mind one will never know. We just grew tired of the nose and eyes bordered by planks of wood and suggested he went home to his mother. He would leave and walk away as far as another gap and there he would stay, nose pushed through and eyes unblinking, until he was moved on yet again.

Then came the night when the occupants of ABC were looked upon in a different light. Gone were the fears that we were a bit out of the ordinary. Help was needed and there was no-one else to call on. One of the girls knocked timidly on the door and when Mother answered it she was surprised to see the hesitant figure and even more curious when a request was made. "Mum wants to know if you can come over?" Well, in the country one does not question requests like that.

"I shan't be a minute," she called in our direction and, throwing on her coat, followed the messenger through the orchard. True to her word she was back in a little longer time than a minute but, nevertheless, only a short while had elapsed. "I've come for something out of the cupboard," she called, carrying one of the oil lamps from the living room through to the scullery. She found the boracic crystals which she was looking for and, returning the lamp to our table, departed once more. A few minutes passed before she came in rather breathlessly and scouted round looking for newspaper, then, taking it with her, off she trod through the orchard yet again. This time she was away for a longer period but we were well occupied and unworried. When she finally arrived home it was past our bedtime and we were hustled upstairs knowing she had been able to help someone who was not well. Next day we discovered Raymond was no longer the baby of that family. Young Winston had arrived! The midwife had been called but haste was not part of her trade and Mother had been summoned in case the midwife arrived after the baby. They must have been extremely grateful for the help Mother had given, for another surprise was in store for us. It was requested, three months later, that Father should be young Winston's Godfather. It was a bolt out of the blue, for no other meetings had taken place between them and us since the night of the baby's arrival. But, as a sign of gratitude on their part, this was the way they felt best able to express it and so we accompanied my father when he joined the family on one of their rare visits to church, knowing he was pleased and happy to comply with their request.

CHAPTER XIV

The hedgerows in summer were a delight to behold, for everywhere one looked there were dog roses, the beautiful yet simple pale pink and white wild roses which grew in profusion, inviting us all to come and smell, come and gather. They had no perfume and should we be tempted to gather we had to be prepared for all the scratches and thorn pricks which inevitably accompanied such an activity. It was not the thought of this discomfort which prevented us from picking them though. We were encouraged to leave the flowers so that their fruits would ripen. As summer gave way to autumn so the roses faded and their fruits, the hips, began to fill out, providing us with another war-effort challenge. When the hips were large and juicy, glowing a delightful orangey-red, the whole class would set off from school in the afternoon, each member armed with a chip (a small cardboard basket). We had a set course to follow and each small group was allotted a hedge. For the whole afternoon, as long as the hips were there for the picking, we picked until our baskets were full and, in the knowledge that we had helped the war effort, we happily returned to school. All the hips were tipped into a large container and were despatched to a centre in town. Our knowledge of the process after this was non-existent but we were told all the fruits were made into syrup, the Rose-Hip Syrup containing the vitamins children needed so much and were prevented from having due to the lack of oranges. These of course, as it was wartime, were not now imported. Rose-hip syrup was a good source of vitamin C for strong growth. It was diluted – a spoonful of syrup in a cup or glass full of water. It was delicious; I enjoyed it.

Of all the seasons, and because of the changes they brought, autumn was my favourite. This was when the spiders' webs glittered with dewdrops among the tall grasses on the roadside. Not content to look and leave, we would pluck a straw from the hedge and crack it in two places, holding the two ends to form a triangle. This framework we held beneath the cobweb and gently raised it, ensuring the complete removal of the web from the hedgerow. In this fashion, armed with a miniature lacrosse racquet, we could study our bejewelled treasure for much longer and, with luck, arrive at school with it intact. I loved being out of doors, close to nature. Autumn had those very special days with their own particular smell. Mother used to stand out in the garden of ABC taking deep breaths and calling "Come and smell the autumn, girls," but at the time I was unimpressed. It must have registered somewhere deep in my memory though for I can "think" that smell! Often nowadays a certain whiff in the air will remind me of that autumn smell. This was the time when the mists were hanging around the orchard, when the sun was a huge golden ball willing its heat to break through the blanket so low on the earth and these were the mornings when we set off to the hop yards.

The army of farmers and their wives, their relatives and their children would emerge from their homes armed with baskets of refreshment, the ladies adorned in aprons beneath their jackets and hats on top of their heads. It could be very hot towards mid-day with no shade overhead. The yards would be standing ready for our onslaught, the vines twisting upwards, heavy with the yellow-green hops. Between the immaculately straight rows of greenery the red earth would be churned into ruts and standing at the beginning of each row was a crib waiting to receive its first consignment. A crib was a large wooden frame, rectangular in shape, onto which sacking had been fixed so that it dipped into the centre. There was a partition half way across thus forming two square cradles and where so desired two people could work one at each end of the crib. If the rows were very long, and this of course depended on the size and length of the field, another crib would be in position at the half-way point, thus indicating that two people should be responsible for that row. Baskets would be placed in the shade beneath the crib, sleeves would be rolled up and knives would be flashing at the ready, for these vines were too tough to break. With a tug they would be brought down from their lofty heights but at the bottom the stem had to be cut. Then, trailing the long vine over the side of the crib and commencing at what was the top, the work would begin of stripping each hop from its stalk among the leaves. The smell was powerful – heavenly. The pollen as one removed the hops would cling to the fingers, turning them a yellowy-brown at the end of the day and how dirty one's fingers became was an indication of the amount of work achieved. As the vines on either side of the crib were stripped, the worker would drag the crib further along the rows. It was fascinating to watch an experienced picker for her fingers moved with the speed of lightning, her hand gradually becoming paralysed with being held in the same position for great lengths of time. Mother was not fast but was of the belief that slow (although not too slow) and steady wins the race.

I would watch for a while, picking here and there, before my attention would be drawn to the livestock – the hop dogs. No, they were not animals but insects which lived in the vines, caterpillars with a difference. They were camouflaged the same colour as the hops, a yellowy-green, with stumpy legs at either end of their long thin hairless bodies. They moved with a great hump in their middle. I watched them for hours, it seemed, until my eye alighted on a chrysalis. These were so beautifully shaped and marked I could not refrain from collecting as many as I could find and placing them in matchboxes for transportation to ABC. Once in the safety of my hiding place I would watch them daily until the moths emerged, dried their wings in the sun and fluttered their thank-yous before disappearing for ever. We would pause in our pursuits mid-morning for the welcome refreshment from the basket, then it was work again till lunchtime. Here Mother showed her true colours for we left the scene and returned home for a break, but the long-standing pickers would again stop only momentarily, preferring to work almost non-stop throughout the day.

There were two periods each day when the general rhythm of the workers gave way to frantic activity, the normal hum being replaced with an air of expectancy as the pickers picked with greater speed if this was at all possible. In the distant rows could be heard a rustling and we knew the owner was doing his round. The aim was always to fill a crib but however hard one tried it always seemed able to take more. Occasionally I would sit beneath it out of the sun and, whereas there was room during the early part of the afternoon, I gradually found my back being supported by the contents as the day wore on. It was our turn for the farmer's inspection and one felt he was judging whether Mother had pulled her weight or not. He would plough a waste-paper type of basket through the hops and bring it out full to the brim, tipping the contents into a sack held open by one of his labourers. "One bushel". Again he filled the basket, "Two," then "Three," and so on until the crib was empty and he marked on Mother's card her number of bushels for the session. At the end of the picking so much was paid for each bushel and, of course, those who wanted more money picked faster!

Each day until the yard was cleared we pursued the same course, with occasional diversions. Elizabeth was at the centre of one of these. As she was sitting on one of the ruts baked hard by the sun, playing with some toys she had brought, she suddenly let out a blood-curdling yell. We were the first to rush to her, wondering what could be the cause. She continued to scream at the top of her voice and other pickers nearby left their work and came to offer assistance, but we did not know where to assist. She was looked all over. She was felt all over. Advice and suggestions came from all directions. Had she fallen and broken her leg? No, those were deemed to be in good working order. What about her arms? They seemed solid enough. Elizabeth continued to scream

127

and we continued to wonder. She gradually responded to Mother's comforting arms and, as her cries died down, the pickers returned to work, anxious not to let too much pay slip through their fingers. Elizabeth began to pat her face and wince at the same time, which localised the trouble, for Mother then observed the cause of the upset, a bee sting near her mouth. As it swelled so she began to panic and wonder how to treat it out there in the hop yard. Now country cures differ from town remedies and "when in Rome do as Rome does!" So the country advice then given was put into action. I ran home for the blue bag. This was a white cotton ankle sock which had had a block of washing blue stuffed into the toe and on wash days it was squeezed into the rinsing water to whiten the whites! No powders with whitening ingredients were available. The blue bag was the answer to the whitest wash. I collected the blue bag, ran it under the pump to wet it and dashed back to the scene of the accident where the country custom was performed of applying the bag to the swollen area. It is doubtful whether any relief was obtained or any value derived from such medication but workers one and all smiled their agreement and work was resumed. Elizabeth seemed to get over her misfortune with no more discomfort so one assumes the right course was followed! It was never put to the test again though.

Tired of watching everyone else and longing for the feel of real money well-earned, I pleaded with my mother to be allowed to have a crib of my own. It was all very well adding hops to her bushels when I felt like it but there was no incentive to work hard and really make my mark. So, after repeated requests, she must have got the message and the day came when I was allocated my own row and my own receptacle. I began when the others began and I worked as fast as my unaccustomed fingers would allow. There was a goal in sight. The breaks I took were half as long as anyone else's. I was out to prove myself and show that when I embarked on something I could see it through. All through that day I picked, not daring to slacken, not wanting anyone to say I had bitten off more than I could chew so when, at the end of the day's labour, the farmer came for his bushels I stood back proudly surveying my efforts – a full crib. The number of bushels was immaterial. It was not conveyed to the memory bank. But the money the bushels represented was very important, for it was wealth indeed to me. Eight shillings and sixpence I had earned. Eight shillings and sixpence which I would be allowed to keep all to myself. That money meant more to me than anything for it was the price of a day's labour, every minute of which I had worked my fingers to the bone in an effort to prove my capabilities, and I had enjoyed it.

CHAPTER XV

News of the raids on the cities was given over the radio and when Father came down to us he brought reports of specific bombings on Birmingham. Three delayed-action bombs had been dropped in the street where Grandmother (on my father's side) lived and where he stayed when he was not away on his travels or with us. But due to the proximity of these bombs the families in this street, as in many others in similar circumstances, had been moved out and Father and his parents were now staying in Hagley. The war was coming closer. So when the sky over the orchard reflected a glow of deep orange and red Mother was afraid. Thoughts raced through her mind of the terror those city folks must be suffering. From the intensity of the glow it would seem a whole city had gone up in flames. She watched in awe as a peculiar light seemed to pervade the earth. It was at the time the sun was setting and, as the sky darkened ominously, she feared it must be the smoke from the fires. An eeriness gathered all around. A creepy feeling ran up and down her spine and, as she watched, fearful though she was yet afraid to move, the sky changed colour. It was no longer aflame with orange and red but emerald, purple and violet creeping over blue. Rooted where she stood she was scared to death, unable to move a limb. As she watched, the colours switched over and under each other. So brilliant were they that words used to describe the scene cannot do it justice. The interplay of light was a sight to behold. "They must be search lights," she thought, "and for them to be searching like that there must be trouble approaching." Never had she felt so scared before. Why, the very trees before her in the orchard had changed colour, their green mossy trunks now appearing deep crimson. It was an illusion. She was going out of her mind. Yet it was magnificent. Minutes afterwards she realised that the colours were fading, that there was no sound to be heard. Even the birds were silent. The glow had almost gone. Surely this was not what she had originally thought. This could not be the result of a raid. This was unearthly. It was a vision. It was a phenomenon. Her fears had subsided somewhat but, with a troubled, wondering mind, she came indoors. She had witnessed something magnificent, if only she knew what. Next morning the newspapers remarked on the phenomenon. What my mother had seen was indeed remarkable as far south as this. She had viewed the Northern Lights, the Aurora Borealis, a sight she was never to forget.

During my earlier sojourn at Mrs. Bourne's I had returned home once for a week-end, no doubt providing a welcome rest for my guardian, and I was treated to the excitement of my first air raid which, in the event, turned out to be just a practice. However, it was real enough for me. To troop downstairs and out through the front door in our night clothes was unheard of. Supposing anyone were to see us? Our next-door neighbours joined in the queue as we passed through the side gate and into the shelter. This was something to tell my friends when I returned to the country. Sitting on the benches along each side of the shelter, which was just large enough for the two families, we waited, straining our ears for sounds of aircraft. Father stood in the doorway looking out and this worried me dreadfully as I thought he would be bombed! The excitement soon began to pall for I was tired, having been woken up from a deep sleep, and the benches were uncomfortable. There was nowhere to lean one's back except against the cold, damp, corrugated iron. The light was dim, just one small candle which wavered and smoked when anyone breathed too hard. As my eyelids began to drop the "all clear" siren brought me back to the present and, while the other occupants were chatting with relief, preparing to return to their beds, I was left rather regretting the peaceful interlude, feeling I had been let down. Nothing, just nothing, had happened.

This night's activity was brought sharply to mind when I heard again the wailing siren, the warning of an air raid. Whereas I was with the family the first time, I was now alone and petrified. I had not long left Mrs. Amies' and was walking home wind-milling the milk when it began. I stopped dead in my tracks, bringing the can of milk abruptly back to earth. What should I do? I was a long way from home. I could never run all the distance in safety. It would be best to retrace my steps to Mrs. Amies' and stay there for a while. If I was not to be safe there I would at least have company! So, as fast as my legs could carry me, I turned and ran. I explained the reason for my return and Mrs. Amies just stared at me in disbelief. She had heard nothing. Well, of course, the siren was in Tenbury, three to four miles away at least and I had only heard it faintly. With all her clattering of pans and cans in the scullery it was no wonder the sound of the warning had not reached her. She came with me out to the garden. There was silence. Of course the warning did not wail for ever. All was calm and serene as usual. "It's alright. You'll come to no harm."

"Please can I stay till the "all clear" goes?"

"Whatever next?" This child was far too conscious of raids. She should never have gone home for that week-end. It had unsettled her. Everyone knew everyone else's business in the country. It was impossible to be away for one night without folk enquiring where, when, why and how.

"Your mother will be wondering where you've got to," she said. "There's no need to worry." I gave her a long look before believing her and when I left her gate I ran every step of the distance between her house and ours, ears straining for any sound, either welcome or otherwise. I arrived home breathless and trembling, pains rearing their heads in every part of my body through the exertion. Mother had heard the warning but she was used to such sounds and paid little attention. As for the "all clear" I did not listen for it any more once I was safe with Mother. My belief that warnings heralded the immediate arrival of enemy aircraft was very naïve. I must control my fears, put them aside and behave normally until action really was demanded.

But when action came I did nothing at all. The first indication of the presence of the enemy came while Mother, my sister and I were sitting in the summer sunshine in the grass at the top of the meadow. The view before us was beautiful. It was so peaceful down there in the haze. It was too nice an afternoon to spend indoors so Mother had brought her knitting while we made daisy chains. From the distance came the sound of an aeroplane, or was it two? As the sound came nearer it gave the impression of speed. We could see nothing for the sound came from above the high summer clouds. Then we knew a chase was on for the "dog fight" was carried out above our heads. The gun shots came in bursts as the attacker tried to capture his prey. It seemed incredible that we should sit there staring upwards hearing it all and straining for just one glimpse of the planes. This was denied us and the pursuer and pursued went on their way. This time there was no evidence to support our story. However, the climax came shortly afterwards. The disturbance outside the cottage early in the morning brought us to the bedroom window. As we looked out we saw people trudging through the orchard and over the gate to the field dipping down to the brook. Some we knew, others were strangers, but the questions we asked ourselves were "Where are they going? What are they doing?" Dressing quickly we were anxious to abate our curiosity and, rushing down the path and through our gate, we bumped into Tom. "What's the trouble? What's going on?" we asked.

"Baint you 'eard?" he replied. "One o' them there Gerries unloaded them bombs last night. Dropped one down there in that field there."

Goodness, it was less than a stone's throw from our cottage. A little bit more to one side and we would have been hit. Figures were standing around a great big hole in the ground. Small children were rushing here and there picking up bits and pieces. This was the most exciting moment of the war! As the enemy planes were being chased by the Air Force they had unloaded their bombs in an effort to lighten the load and add speed in their attempt to escape. One stray bomb had found its way into the nearby field and all that was left was the hole at which the country folk were staring in wonder, and bits of shrapnel which the children were collecting for souvenirs. We had had no warning siren! We had heard no explosion! And this was the nearest contact we, and the surrounding country folk, had with the war.

My second return to the city was unavoidable since Mother and Father had some business to attend to and we had to accompany them. By now private cars had been taken off the road and only official cars with special dispensation were allowed to run. However, motorbikes were given a further three months' reprieve since their petrol consumption was far less. The slogan "Is your journey really necessary?" was a constant reminder of the shortage of petrol and other fuels. Since Father was anxious to continue his visits to us some way had to be found and, after much thought, he arrived at the decision to buy a three-wheeled car, for this type of vehicle was classed, not as a car, but as a motorbike. Full of beans, he arrived in this three-wheeler but, when Mother looked inside and counted two seats, she wondered how it was possible to fit in four bodies. Nevertheless, where there's a will there's a way, and, packed like sardines in a can, Mother, Father, Elizabeth and I, complete with luggage, managed to find just enough room to close both doors. With a wiggle and a giggle we made ourselves comfortable for the journey to Birmingham, for once we had begun there would be no chance of stretching our legs or moving our position. Everything went as planned. Nothing untoward occurred and we started our journey back to ABC. Travelling at night time was hazardous and watching Father as he drove I was full of admiration. For fear of attracting enemy aircraft all headlights had to be fitted with masks. These were like Venetian blinds, permanently at an angle, and so very little light came through them to show the way ahead. It must have been a terrible strain on the driver peering to see the road just in front of his vehicle. All white lines had been removed so that when our island was invaded the enemy would derive no help from that quarter. Cats' eyes were as yet unheard of. There were no street lights in the towns or cities and all houses had to be blacked out so the driver needed to know every inch of the road if he were to arrive at his destination safely. I believe my father was one of that category and, as he drove us along in silence, I too tried to memorise the route. We were bobbing along very comfortably, at least as comfortably as could be expected in such cramped conditions, when a light was flashed in front of us. A dim light it was. It seemed like a torch. We slowed down and came to a halt. "What's the matter?" Mother's question was directed at Father and her voice sounded very hoarse.

"Police checking up on cars and their occupants."

"They'll summons us for overloading," she whispered, looking at the four of us sitting on two seats. "They'll say you're driving dangerously, not under proper control."

"They won't."

Then Mother turned to me. "Make yourself as small as possible." Goodness, I could not move an inch. "The car's too heavily laden. It's too low on the ground. They'll tell us we can't continue. Girls, make yourselves as light as possible."

I breathed in, sure this would help.

"Don't worry," whispered Father. "Leave it to me." But Mother was worried no matter how reassuring Father's words were meant to be. A hand was placed on the low bonnet and a torch light shone through the celluloid window.

"Turn the window down," said Father and Mother managed to move her arm sufficiently to allow the window winder to turn. The light flashed in each of our four white faces, then again in reverse as though the owner couldn't quite take in what he saw. Seconds passed as he seemed to weigh up the situation while we all felt our blood running cold.

The light returned to Father and a voice behind it asked "Where are you going and what is your reason? No cars are allowed unless on essential business," which obviously we were not. We were caught red-handed, as it were.

Father, unknown to us, must have been prepared for such an event because he calmly answered the constable in very distinct tones "I'm three-wheeler class. We're classed as a motorbike, not a car." The torch quickly flashed along the side of the car as if to verify the statement. Perhaps the constable had been taken by surprise by this answer for he made no comment about overloading or dangerous driving conditions. He realised the truth of Father's statement and, with a salute and a smile in his voice, he apologised for the delay.

"Oh, sorry sir. Carry on."

As the car, or motorbike, call it what you will – we preferred "three-wheeler" – began to move we all let out a long sigh. Relief swept over us and we all felt ourselves relaxing. "There's a fish-and-chip shop not far away. Anyone hungry?" asked the driver and, after he had treated us, we sat in a country lane in the dark, eating our chips and feeling for the bones in our fish. We heard the wailing warning. We saw lights in the sky from the searchlights as their beams crisscrossed over each other seeking the enemy planes, and we continued eating our chips! What mattered was that we were all together and when the "all clear" siren went we could continue our homeward journey.

CHAPTER XVI

Winter came with a vengeance. These winters in England were renowned for their severity and we had known nothing quite like them before. As we began to feel a nip in the air our eyes would stray beyond the orchard, beyond the fields to the hills in the far distance. These were the Clee Hills and we were anxiously watching the summit each day. The first hint of white on the top was an indication that snow was on the way, our warning to be prepared. Beneath the trees in the orchard the grass was velvety, from the cottage half way towards the gate that is. Then it gradually deteriorated for where the vehicles came through, the bikes and the tradesmen's vans as well as farm machinery, the ground was churned up into a quagmire. The summer suns dried up all the moisture and we walked on the hard-baked ruts; to step in between was to invite a sprained ankle, walking on the top was dare-devilish, but at least if you injured yourself falling into a rut it was more excusable than purposely stepping into it! When the rain came this area became a sea of mud and it was impossible to find a suitable foothold. Even by walking on the grass to the hedge and working along towards the gate that way was little better, for one still had to hang on to the branches, body positioned as for rock-climbing up a sheer face, in order to navigate the opening. Wellingtons were a must and after returning from a paddle the accustomed method of cleaning up was to stand facing the pump, feet under the spout, and pump till one was drenched! We were then certain to be free of mud.

ABC showing the pump with Elizabeth and Aunt Maud

So it is not surprising that for three-quarters of the year we left the cottage wearing wellingtons. One looked rather odd if one was otherwise dressed for visiting or for town, but an observant onlooker would be aware of the fact that we all carried our shoes. No matter what else we had, be it basket, brolly or bag, no matter whether we were dressed in our best or our worst outfits, we all carried shoes. We plodded and sucked our way through the mud to the gate and, hanging on for all we were worth, we opened it, our feet sliding this way and that, till the last one was through and it was securely fastened behind us. A further balancing act to get clear of it on the other side and then we stopped. Off came the wellingtons, hands becoming caked in mud as we struggled to remove them, and on went the shoes. We used the long, wet grass nearby to clean the mud off our hands before we set off on our mission, leaving a strange sight behind us. There, hanging in the branches of the trees, dangling in the wind, were at least six wellington boots! We knew that however long we left them there no-one would take them and that they would still be there waiting to serve us on our return trip through the orchard.

Father never brought his transport up to the cottage. He would leave it outside the orchard gate if the ground was too boggy and come just inside the gate when it was dry. Once stuck in that mud the wheels would spin round and round and there would be little hope of escaping without assistance and this was not very forthcoming. Feeling some attempt ought to be made to ease the problem, Father set to work whenever he came down at the week-ends. The brook at the bottom of the field on the gate side of the orchard had a good deal of gravel and stones in its bed and, armed with spade and wheelbarrow, he set off to reclaim it. It was hard work, especially pushing a full, heavy barrow back up the sloping field. A shovelful at a time he placed it on the mud and, when a firm enough patch had been laid, he would stamp it home, but it was a slow process and took innumerable days of tireless effort to show little progress. Nevertheless, his work was appreciated by all who had to trudge that way. The tradesmen commented on the improvement and so did the farmer. I wonder why it is that farmers always prefer to wallow in mud!

The snows followed. A hint of snow on one day would be followed by a heavy fall during the night and the next day we would be imprisoned. It was a delightful sight which greeted us as we looked through the bedroom window on just such a morning. The sloping field would no longer slope, the mud at the gate had disappeared under a thick white blanket and the bare branches of the trees were bowing low under their burden. We knew that to open the front door would be to start an avalanche, for the prevailing wind drifted the snow right up to the roof. After removing the blackout the rooms downstairs remained in darkness because of the height of the drift. This is why we continually looked towards the Clee, for the advance warning we received gave us time to bring indoors all brooms, shovels and home-made "snow-movers" which were normally stored in the outhouse. Gingerly opening the door we then had to begin to tunnel our way out till we were clear of the drift then, from that end, we could attack the snow and clear the doorway and the window. But this was only the beginning. The toilet was round the back and a path had to be cleared in that direction before digging through to our gate into the orchard. Wellingtons were hardly of use to us now but they had to do as we had nothing better. One step out into the orchard and our feet would sink into the snow till it was way past our knees. Our boots would fill with snow with each step we took and our journey to school would take twice as long, for every few steps we took we had to unload. The exercise was marvellous, our knees reaching to our chins in an effort to place one foot in front of the other. But we never thought of staying at home. We were late for school. It was inevitable, for who could blame us for snowballing each other as we met. Our clothes would be soaked but the fire-guard in the classroom was large enough to cope with the worst. Our boots we stood upside down in the corner of the room with miniature rivers emerging from underneath.

Alas, much as we enjoyed the fun, our parents had other problems. When the snow was as deep as this here the tradesmen were unable to reach these outlying districts and for days the cottages would be isolated. The telephone wires were down, the roads were impassable and fetching the milk was a nightmare. On occasions when we could not get to Mrs. Amies' the farmer who owned ABC let us have some of his milk and to reach his farm a way had to be cut through the blocks of snow. Passing through was like being enclosed between two brilliant white walls.

The week-end arrived, and so did Uncle Howard. He had travelled down on the Friday night, accompanied by a friend, to the farm way over Pigeon Hill. By the Saturday the snow had come to stay and he viewed the scene with disquiet. He had to return to work on Monday and his car was already snowed in so he decided to trudge over to the cottage to see if Father had arrived, hoping they would both be able to travel back with him. He was welcomed by my mother and was offered refreshment and a warm by the fire but it was obvious that he had something else on his mind.

"Where's Albert then?" he asked, having noted Father's absence.

"He's not here," replied Mother.

"What time's he due?"

"Oh, I'm not expecting him this week-end, not in weather like this!" Uncle Howard's face fell. How on earth was he going to get out of this God-forsaken place? Shortly after receiving the information he didn't want to hear, he took his leave to trudge again over his tracks on Pigeon Hill and we settled down to a week-end on our own. It was lunchtime on the Sunday, after a further fall of snow, that Father arrived on the doorstep. We shrieked with joy but what had happened? How was it that he arrived so late? He was very late finishing work on the Saturday and, as the state of the roads was so bad, he had delayed setting off until early on Sunday morning, not wishing to struggle through in the dark. He had travelled reasonably well till he reached Aston Bank then he met a wall of snow. That was it! Very wisely he never went on a journey without his tools which always included a spade so, having weighed up the prospects, he decided to leave his car in an opening down on the main road and set off, spade at the ready, to dig his way through. This he had just accomplished. During lunch Mother told him of his cousin's visit and immediately after he had finished his meal Mother and Father set out on the track over the hill to call on Uncle Howard and make arrangements for their return on the morrow. As Father's car was at the bottom of Aston Bank and Uncle's nearest way to the main road joined it at the second junction beyond this, it was agreed each would make his own way to the main road for a certain time and Father would pick up the two of them, Uncle Howard and his friend. Accordingly, on Monday morning he set off, while the snow which was still falling settled in each footprint that he left. The drifts were insurmountable. As he was wondering what he should do next our next-door neighbour appeared, his wellington boots topped by sacking tied up with string reaching right up to the top of his thighs. "You won't get through that way," he told Father. "Better follow me," and he led the way over the fields where he knew from experience that the drifts were not so deep. Eventually the main road was reached and Father set off towards Birmingham, wipers struggling to clear the snow which was clinging ever more forcefully to the window. As he struggled with the steering wheel to keep the wheels turning and the car moving his eyes were peering through the screen for the sight of his two fellow travellers. There was only one man anywhere to be seen walking in the same direction, hands shoved deep in his pockets, hat well over his eyes, head bent low to protect himself from the driving snow and Father drove on still searching but there was not a soul in sight. As he glanced through the driving mirror a running, stumbling figure appeared behind in the distance, arms waving madly, trying to attract his attention. Another closer look through the mirror revealed the man in the hat, his hands no longer stuffed in his pockets. Good Gracious! It was Howard. Father had passed him by and, as he had done so, Howard had been panic stricken to see his would-be transport disappearing before his eyes in the distance. Albert had not recognised him. He was desperate in his attempts to attract his attention but Father had been looking for two men. When at last Howard caught up, breathless, cold and exhausted, he explained that his friend had thought better of returning by car in such conditions and had caught the early morning train back. One can understand the friend's discomfort and surprise when he found himself back in Birmingham half an hour after the car travellers!

During this particularly bad period we had been cut off for almost ten days. Stores were getting low, food was getting scarce and we wondered how much longer we could hold out. It was obvious when Gertie and her sister Grace arrived at our door that they could manage no longer. "We wondered if you have a spade which you could lend us?

We've got one but we each need one. We've got to get some supplies, we've no bread nor meat. We're going to dig through to Tenbury."

"Dig through to Tenbury?" My mother was astounded. "It's over three and a half miles. You'll never get through. You'll never get that far!"

"Well, we'll try. We'll get as far as we can. If we reach the bottom of Aston Bank perhaps we'll find the main road open." So, armed with a spade each, they began to dig and, before long, they disappeared from view. They made it! They dug what looked like a trench along the centre of the road through the snow which was shoulder high, clearing enough to enable someone on foot to pass through. They reached the main road, halfway to Tenbury, relieved to find traffic could at least travel this far, albeit with great difficulty.

It was a great time for us children. We snowballed and built gigantic snowmen which lasted for weeks but best of all were the toboggan runs. The meadow provided the most perfect setting and children and parents congregated at the top of the hill to begin the long run down to the brook where the king-cups grew. Fortunately for us, the meadow levelled out before reaching the boggy ground so we were certain of pulling up well before that. Half a dozen runs would be used at a time giving us ample opportunity to race each other to the bottom, the best races being those when we were two up on a toboggan. My favourite companion of course was George. He was older than most of us and knew how to guide us straight to the bottom whereas, left to our own endeavours, our sledge went by any route but the most direct, generally dropping us off at the halfway stage. It was dark in the evening when we started sledging and by the time we finished the moon would be high in the sky, bathing everywhere in a greenish light. We were never ready to leave the slope when the time came to return home and prepare for bed. It was so exhilarating out there in the moonlight but I dare say Mother recognised our tiredness before we were conscious of it and we finally gave in to the enticement of a cup of hot cocoa in front of the fire before climbing exhausted but happy into bed.

The snow stayed with us for a very long time and we grew accustomed to the slow progress we were forced to make while going about our business. We still had to get into town so, as usual on a Saturday morning, we trod out the long, long road. The hard-packed snow where people had walked provided a fairly firm foothold as we passed under the firs bordering this stretch. During the summer and autumn we had stood here in silence, gazing upward into the trees, while the squirrels entertained us with their antics, leaping and bounding from branch to branch, tails stretched out behind them. They had more sense than to put their noses out of their dreys at this time of the year and we knew it was no good looking for them although our gaze wandered upward automatically. We lived in hope.

It was while Mother and Elizabeth were thus occupied that I disappeared – unintentionally and very unexpectedly of course! One always delights in treading where no man has trod before, referring to snow that is, and I was no exception. On the contrary, I was always first there. So, seeing a delightful area of snow sporting not one single footprint, I took a flying leap. One minute I was there, the next I had gone. The only indication of my presence was a round hole where before there was not a footprint – which goes to show everyone had more sense than I. Down, down I had gone to the bottom of a six-foot drift and not even a hair on my head could be seen. My surprise was so great that for a second or two I was dumbfounded. A muffled call for help brought Mother's attention back to the present and, looking around, she was mystified both by the call and my disappearance. "I'm in here. Help!" Like a mole burrowing underground and throwing up the soil, leaving mole hills behind him, I was trying unsuccessfully to help myself. The seemingly self-propelled snow brought Mother to the edge of the drift. It was fortunate that the land sloped for, as she caught my hands and tugged, I was able to scramble out and, after being brushed down and quizzed as to the state of my limbs, we continued on our way. I had learnt my lesson. Never again would I tread undented snow without first testing it to make sure there was firm ground underneath.

CHAPTER XVII

"Please can we go through Boraston?" was our constant request whenever we were fortunate enough to accompany Father in the car. Boraston was a tiny hamlet reached by the lane which turned right outside the orchard gate. We never walked down there. We never had cause to for there was nothing at Boraston except a house or two, yet both Mother and Father knew the attraction. Mother liked to go this way into Tenbury. It was further round than the usual way and met the main road by the Peacock Inn, the drop down to the road being equally as sheer and hazardous as Aston Bank. Mother's hobby was looking at houses and, while she delighted in first these windows and then those chimneys, my thoughts were far away, interrupted only by a grunt or an agreement when her comments required recognition. This lane dropped to the level of the brook from which Father had removed half its bed. I suppose when the road had first been constructed there was a shortage of money for they had not been able to build a bridge and therefore the road ran right under the water! There was no knowing how the workmen were able to achieve this feat but it was there for all to see. This was the reason for our request to go via this route. As the lane ran straight downhill into the water we always urged Father to use it like a race track. "Go fast. Go faster." We would bounce up and down at the back of the car trying to give it added impetus for the faster we went down the lane, the harder we would hit the water and the greater the spray we would send up on both sides of the car.

Boraston ford

But, persist as we would in our efforts to beat the clock Father rarely went more than "too slow." We still made a splash but it never came up to our expectations. We just knew we could give a better display than that. Of course, we gave no consideration to the fact that the lane was only wide enough for one car. There were no passing places so if we met a vehicle coming in the other direction we must needs reverse and, as we were on the downward run, it would inevitably mean us going back to the top. Neither did we consider the workings of the car for it did not worry us that the water might get into the exhaust pipe or, if the brook was high, that the water would seep into the car.

Mother's interest in houses was not an idle pastime for, unknown to us, she and my father were looking around for other accommodation. The farmer had decided to sell and along with the farm and the fields went the orchard and the cottage, for the prospective buyer insisted on having ABC for his workman. Father was given notice to quit. Our own house back in the city had been let to a family whose work was there and this arrangement suited us down to the ground until we wanted to move back again. The bombings were over, the war was receding from our islands and, when the farmer notified my father of his intention to sell and the complications that were involved, it was time to reclaim our property, but the tenants had no desire to move. For that matter, Mother had no desire to return and viewed every house in the vicinity if she thought there was the slightest chance of acquiring it. At the same time Father frequently called to ask what arrangements his tenants in Birmingham had made and was constantly told "None." He set to work to find other accommodation for them to rent, to let, or to buy and presented them with the information he had collected until they had no answer to his plea to move out since time was getting short for us. The new owner of the farm was close on our heels, wondering how soon it would be before he could install his labourer.

There was an air of expectancy surrounding our removal back to Birmingham. I would return to my old school, play with my old friends, visit all the people I knew so well. We would be near the shops. There were buses to town. In fact, life would be very much easier. No more pumping water. What fun it would be to turn on a tap! A bath – we could have a bath immediately with hot water from the immersion heater. There would be no need to go outside in all weathers to "spend a penny" and Mother would no longer have to fight with the copper or saw logs for the fire. We were going home at last. No two girls could have been more excited than Elizabeth and myself but the excitement vanished into thin air after we had settled in. It was all so strange here. It was different. I did not like it one bit. We could not go out into the orchard any more. We were not free any longer. Everywhere seemed so crowded in on us. It was horrible. Inevitably, I shed a tear and this was the opening of the flood gates! I cried and cried and cried. For three days I wept and all that my parents could get out of me was "I want to go back home. This is not my real home. Please take me back to the country. Please take me home." For one ten-year-old girl life had changed for the worse. I had left home as an evacuee, just as many others had done, not knowing where I would land, and now, four years later, I had returned regretfully to that home. Given the same opportunities again I would accept them gladly with open arms, for my life was now richer by far for all the experiences of my country life in wartime.

We have been back to Aston Bank occasionally over the years but changes have been made. ABC is still there but it has been renamed "Cherry Tree Cottage" and is now a Grade II listed building. Alas, the orchard is no longer there, and the school has closed and is now a private dwelling. We no longer rest our arms on the top of the gate and lean over, looking into space, for no-one watching could see what we see. Their dreams are not our dreams. All that is now left of those wonderful years are the memories.

Ann Yardley, Knighton-on-Teme School

Betty Albeard, Sheila Henderson and me on a log.
The log where I am sitting behind Sheila Henderson with Betty Albeard
in front is at the cross roads below New Inn, found on the left.

Taking the road back up the hill behind the photographer (my father), we pass, on the left, the cottage where Gertie Cox lived. Further up the hill, under the hedge, the lords and ladies (arums) could be found. At the top right is ABC which is now known as "Cherry Tree Cottage", and on the left is our landlord's farm, the Moore's farm, where Tom lived with his father, in the picture it is Aston Bank Farm.

Continuing over the top of the hill and down the lane opposite we come to the ford and Boraston.

From Moore's farm, along the road on the left, we pass Aston Court on the left and further along, on the right, the field where the army camp was situated at the top of Aston Bank. At the bottom of Aston Bank we meet the road to Tenbury and to the dancing class.

Back now to the log, on the left of which is the copse where the king cups grew, and to the near left is the meadow where we tobogganed and heard the planes in the dog fight. At the top is ABC in the cherry orchard.

The road leading forward from the log passes, on the left, the houses where George Randle and Derek Wilcox lived, and on the right, Peg's cottage, which can just be seen in the photograph. The road leads on to New Inn where Elma Mees lived, then on to Little London and Long Length.

At the log again, the signpost points to Jewkes Lane where we pass Mr. Went's cottage on the right, deep in the trees, Pigeon Hill on the left and on to the pool and Maes Court. Mrs. Amies' is on the opposite corner and this road to the left leads to High Hall and Mrs. Bourne's to where I was evacuated, shown as Woodgates Green on the map.

At Maes Court, cross straight over, down the hill, past the Rectory and on to Knighton Church and Adams' farm, along the gated road and up the hill to reach the road to Knighton School.

Acknowledgements

My thanks to Jane McIntosh for editing this book and for her valuable help and advice.

Much appreciation also for the help given by the many friends made during the compiling of up-to-date photographs, especially Sheila Bragger.

Thanks also to Judy Wright for permission to use her delightfully illustrated map of Knighton-on-Teme.

My greatest thanks to my sister Jane who has given her time and energy so generously in order to bring this book to fruition.

And thanks to Ann Wallace for her assistance in publishing this book as well as the designing and formatting of the book cover.

Made in the USA
Charleston, SC
14 July 2016